Creating Distinctiveness:
Lessons from Uncommon Colleges and Universities

by Barbara K. Townsend, L. Jackson Newell, and Michael D. Wiese

ASHE-ERIC Higher Education Report No. 6, 1992

Prepared by

Clearinghouse on Higher Education
The George Washington University

In cooperation with

Association for the Study
of Higher Education

Published by

School of Education and Human Development
The George Washington University

Jonathan D. Fife, Series Editor

Cite as

Townsend, Barbara K., L. Jackson Newell, and Michael D. Wiese. 1992. *Creating Distinctiveness: Lessons from Uncommon Colleges and Universities.* ASHE-ERIC Higher Education Report No. 6. Washington, D.C.: The George Washington University, School of Education and Human Development.

Library of Congress Catalog Card Number 93-83928
ISSN 0884-0040
ISBN 1-878380-19-2

Managing Editor: Bryan Hollister
Manuscript Editor: Alexandra Rockey
Cover design by Michael David Brown, Rockville, Maryland

The ERIC Clearinghouse on Higher Education invites individuals to submit proposals for writing monographs for the *ASHE-ERIC Higher Education Report* series. Proposals must include:
1. A detailed manuscript proposal of not more than five pages.
2. A chapter-by-chapter outline.
3. A 75-word summary to be used by several review committees for the initial screening and rating of each proposal.
4. A vita and a writing sample.

ERIC **Clearinghouse on Higher Education**
School of Education and Human Development
The George Washington University
One Dupont Circle, Suite 630
Washington, DC 20036-1183

This publication was prepared partially with funding from the Office of Educational Research and Improvement, U.S. Department of Education, under contract no. ED RI-88-062014. The opinions expressed in this report do not necessarily reflect the positions or policies of OERI or the Department.

EXECUTIVE SUMMARY

There is a sameness about the undergraduate programs of many of America's colleges and universities, despite their many differences in origin, size, and location. Even so, most define themselves as unique by emphasizing a particular program here or an unusual characteristic there. Yet few stray far from the basic patterns that define their missions, organize their faculties, and structure their curricula.

A few colleges and universities, however, are fundamentally different. We call these distinctive institutions and are fascinated by their origins and practices, for they remind us that significant educational innovations can be initiated and sustained.

What Is Institutional Distinctiveness?

Distinctive colleges and universities share certain characteristics: a unifying theme or vision of what education should be, the expression of this theme or vision in all or most institutional activities, and the striving for excellence to achieve their purpose.

Ultimately, the distinctive institution is a product of a social contract among colleagues to organize their efforts around a unifying purpose. Institutional distinctiveness results when both internal and external constituents support the values and vision that drive a college or university's curriculum and educational practices (Clark 1970; Kuh and Whitt 1988).

What Lessons Can We Learn from Distinctive Colleges?

Distinctive schools often develop in response to newly emerging societal or community needs unmet by existing colleges and universities. Witness the founding of Berea College inspired by the educational needs of Appalachians or Deep Springs founded to develop national leaders. They may also develop from strains within academe itself, as was the case when Alexander Meiklejohn founded the Experimental College at the University of Wisconsin or Robert Hutchins the undergraduate College at the University of Chicago. Threat of collapse or university failure also can precipitate a college developing a distinctive educational philosophy, as the history of St. John's indicates.

Not all distinctive colleges endure. Some such as Antioch have a long history of distinctiveness, while others such as Black Mountain College are an experiment that does not endure. Some are highly prescriptive, while others give students almost unlimited academic choice. Some follow a progressive or whole-person approach, while others advocate an intellectual or neo-classical philosophy of education.

The educational program of some schools such as the College of the Atlantic draws fully upon its geographical setting, while others such as St. John's take no heed. Regardless of their life span, degree of prescriptiveness, educational philosophy, or setting, distinctive colleges challenge conventional ideas about higher education and inspire us to engage both students and faculty more fully in undergraduate education.

What Are the Lures and Perils of Distinctiveness?

Institutional distinctiveness is an appealing yet elusive concept that suggests uncommon leadership and institutional excellence. Distinctive colleges and universities often have prospective students and faculty clamoring to join. Once there, they find an *esprit de corps* that often makes their lives more enjoyable and also aids in promotion and development activities and in making management decisions.

Distinctiveness also has its perils. Being highly distinctive can hurt an institution, primarily by limiting it to a very small market niche. Also, the very values that unify the college may work as a constraint against further change necessary for survival.

Few colleges and universities find it easy to be distinctive. Certain factors such as public control, lack of external support for an institution's guiding vision, the expectations of regional and programmatic accrediting associations, and standardized norms for excellence may serve to inhibit developing distinctive educational practices.

What Strategic Management Models May Lead to Distinctiveness?

Commitment to a particular educational "calling" does not assure that students will enroll and that foundations and individuals will donate money. Visionaries and idealists may benefit from strategic management techniques to help ensure the success of colleges and universities.

Strategic management literature reflects two major models: the adaptive and the interpretive (Chaffee 1984). Adherence to the adaptive model, which emphasizes resource acquisition, environmental realities, and market trends, may produce competitive advantage in the marketplace without creating institutional distinctiveness. In contrast, the interpretive model's emphasis on articulating values and developing a culture warranting individuals' commitment may ignore market realities in the highly competitive world of higher education.

The Porter Generic Model (Porter 1985) is a commonly used model for organizing business strategies. When applied to strategic management decisions, the model illustrates how colleges and universities can differentiate themselves and gain a competitive edge. However, this approach will not produce institutional distinctiveness. In the long run the truly distinctive school is likely to result from a merging of both the paradigms.

What Recommendations Can Be Made To Leaders and Researchers?

Higher education leaders contemplating whether to pursue distinctiveness can follow a six-step plan to determine the viability of the strategy. Although the plan uses the tools of adaptive strategic management, ultimately the strategy is based on the interpretive model of management.

1. Conduct historical and cultural analyses to uncover institutional values.
2. Make a paradigm check to determine which strategic management model guides their own and their institution's actions.
3. Clarify, communicate, and act on unifying values and themes.
4. Conduct a situation analysis to determine if the current state of the college or university makes it a likely candidate for distinctiveness.
5. Select the desired level of market exposure, whether it be local, regional, or national.
6. Execute market research to uncover markets to which the college or university's values and educational vision may appeal.

Combining the tools of adaptive management with the perspective of interpretive management increases the likelihood that a distinctive college or university will not only survive but indeed thrive in the marketplace. While the benefits of attending a distinctive college or university have not been well researched, it appears that students, as well as faculty and indeed the entire system of higher education, benefit from the existence of distinctive schools (Townsend 1989).

ADVISORY BOARD

Barbara E. Brittingham
The University of Rhode Island

Jay L. Chronister
University of Virginia

Carol Everly Floyd
Board of Regents of the Regency Universities System
State of Illinois

Rodolfo Z. Garcia
Michigan State University

Elizabeth M. Hawthorne
University of Toledo

L. Jackson Newell
University of Utah

Barbara Taylor
Association of Governing Boards of Universities and Colleges

CONSULTING EDITORS

Philip Altbach
State University of New York–Buffalo

A. Nancy Avakian
Metropolitan State University

Margaret J. Barr
Texas Christian University

Beverly Belson
Western Michigan University

David W. Breneman
Harvard University

Barbara B. Burn
University of Massachusetts–Amherst

L. Edwin Coate
Oregon State University

Robert Cope
Northwoods Institute

John W. Creswell
University of Nebraska–Lincoln

Dennis E. Gregory
Wake Forest University

Robert M. Hendrickson
The Pennsylvania State University

Mary Ann Heverly
Delaware County Community College

Malcolm D. Hill
The Pennsylvania State University

Edward R. Hines
Illinois State University

Clifford P. Hooker
University of Minnesota

Donald Hossler
Indiana University

Joan Isenberg
George Mason University

Donald Kirby
Le Moyne College

REVIEW PANEL

Charles Adams
University of Massachusetts–Amherst

Louis Albert
American Association for Higher Education

Richard Alfred
University of Michigan

Philip G. Altbach
State University of New York–Buffalo

Marilyn J. Amey
University of Kansas

Louis C. Attinasi, Jr.
University of Houston

Robert J. Barak
Iowa State Board of Regents

Alan Bayer
Virginia Polytechnic Institute and State University

John P. Bean
Indiana University

Louis W. Bender
Florida State University

John M. Braxton
Vanderbilt University

Peter McE. Buchanan
Council for Advancement and
    Support of Education

John A. Centra
Syracuse University

Arthur W. Chickering
George Mason University

Shirley M. Clark
Oregon State System of Higher Education

Darrel A. Clowes
Virginia Polytechnic Institute and State University

John W. Creswell
University of Nebraska–Lincoln

Deborah DiCroce
Piedmont Virginia Community College

Richard Duran
University of California

Kenneth C. Green
University of Southern California

Edward R. Hines
Illinois State University

Marsha W. Krotseng
West Virginia State College and University Systems

George D. Kuh
Indiana University–Bloomington

Daniel T. Layzell
University of Wisconsin System

Meredith Ludwig
American Association of State Colleges and Universities

Mantha V. Mehallis
Florida Atlantic University

Robert J. Menges
Northwestern University

Toby Milton
Essex Community College

James R. Mingle
State Higher Education Executive Officers

Gary Rhoades
University of Arizona

G. Jeremiah Ryan
Harford Community College

Daryl G. Smith
Claremont Graduate School

William Tierney
Pennsylvania State University

Susan Twombly
University of Kansas

Harold Wechsler
University of Rochester

Michael J. Worth
George Washington University

CONTENTS

FOREWORD

In many respects, all colleges and academic programs are unique, since no two institutions or faculty are alike. However, being "one of a kind" and being distinctive is not the same. Generally, something is considered distinctive if it has one or more of the following characteristics: stands out as being not only different, but better; excels in serving an obviously desired need; is more effective in achieving its end; and has a style or process that is not used by others. In other words, distinctiveness occurs when something is perceived as being uniquely better than what exists.

If most colleges believe their programs are significantly different from corresponding programs at other colleges, then why are not more programs considered distinctive? The answer lies in having a distinctive vision and the courage to do things differently to follow that vision.

Part of the motivating force behind the creation of a distinctive vision is a sense that something is missing that is preventing achieving an end goal. In most cases, the goal or mission of a distinctive program is not terribly different than the average program, but the approach is.

One characteristic that distinguishes distinctive programs is the clarity of their vision. This clarity comes from one or more persons championing that vision until others internalize the vision and it becomes their own. They, in turn, convince others of the wisdom of their vision. The enthusiasm of these leaders are contagious, and others are persuaded that the benefits of the vision outweigh the risks of doing something different. As others join the process and further discuss the vision, there develops a sense of purpose or *raison d'etre* that provides an intense, passionate focus resulting in the courage to act. Thus, a distinctive program is born.

While distinctive programs seem to flourish when they are relatively unknown, with visibility they experience increased pressure to return to the "normal" way of doing things. Over time, most distinctive programs do not survive, mainly because the education policy and power structure are uncomfortable with truly different programs. Whether it be other faculty within the institution, legislators, accrediting agencies, or certification boards, there is a tendency to feel that if it differs from what has been done in the past, it may not work.

Therefore, at best, there is a demand that distinctive programs prove that they accomplish what they claim. Since the champions of these programs are much more concerned with following their vision, formal assessment of these programs seldom occurs. When the champion finally moves on, the program soon either is discontinued or reverts back to more common ways of conducting business.

The question remains: How can programs and institutions become distinct and maintain a sense of distinctiveness over time? In this report by Barbara K. Townsend, associate professor, Loyola University Chicago; L. Jackson Newell, professor, University of Utah; and Michael D. Wiese, associate professor, Anderson University, the concept of distinctiveness is reviewed. The authors carefully set the stage by identifying the characteristics of distinctiveness. Then, in great detail, the authors examine the history of many notable programs and institutions. This history clearly demonstrates the advantages and disadvantages that these institutions experienced. A final and most important question analyzed by the authors: How can programs or institutions become more effectively distinctive?

By using their unique strengths and focused vision, every higher education program or institution has the capacity to become distinctive. This report addresses what this means, how great the risks and rewards, and what needs to be done to make this distinctiveness long lived. To what degree this direction is appropriate for a specific institution's mission only can be decided after all the considerations are reviewed. This report will greatly assist in that process.

Jonathan D. Fife
Series Editor, Professor of Higher Education Administration, and Director, ERIC Clearinghouse on Higher Education

ACKNOWLEDGMENTS

The authors wish to thank graduate assistants Celia Bergman, Cecelia Corey, and Katherine Reynolds for their help in preparing this manuscript. The authors also wish to thank the following graduate students for their assistance in studying the colleges described in Chapter 2: Ann Adams, Clifford Crelly, Kerrie Naylor, Zandile Nkabinde, Richard Sperry, Ryo Takahashi, Barbra Wardle, and Keith Wilson.

PINNING DOWN AN ELUSIVE CONCEPT

Like snowflakes viewed through a magnifying glass, colleges and universities viewed through the lens of organizational culture display unique patterns that are immensely intriguing to institutional members and make for good reading for higher education scholars. The same snowflakes viewed through a motorist's windshield look very much alike.

So, too, do colleges and universities seem typical when viewed from a systemic perspective. Standardized in conformance with regional accrediting criteria and state board regulations, partly to ensure student and faculty ease in transferring from institution to institution, higher education institutions exhibit remarkable homogeneity in basic missions and educational agendas.

There are exceptions. We call these exceptions "distinctive institutions" and argue that they can accurately lay claim to being out of the ordinary, as the word "distinctive" commonly is understood to mean. We value these exceptions, for they serve as alternative visions of higher education, prompting others to rethink what their school can be and who it can well serve.

An example drawn from the development of English universities illustrates this point. In the early 1800s, Oxford and Cambridge awarded degrees only to students who were in good standing with the Church of England. Growing religious and cultural diversity within British society, precipitated by increasing industrialization and a global empire, meant that many Evangelical Protestants, Jews, Dissenters, and others outside the established church had the means and desire for a university education. When Oxford and Cambridge remained unresponsive to the new demand, London University opened in the 1820s to qualified students, regardless of their religious beliefs.

A distinctive departure from academic norms of its day, London University staked out religious tolerance and the separation of scientific and theological thinking as hallmarks of its bold mission. The new London University was immediately assailed by "Oxbridge" dons and by established political and religious leaders. However, although London University's innovations began as heresies, they shortly became orthodoxies in British higher education (Clive and Pinney, eds. 1972). London University's story is just one example of the influence distinctive colleges and universities can have on the larger systems of which they are a part.

What makes some colleges and universities distinctive is not clearly understood. Some college and university leaders may assume their schools are distinctive because they are different from any other. Similarly, legislators and other state-level officials examining their state's higher education system may confuse institutional variety with distinctiveness.

Assuming distinctiveness where there is merely diversity or simple difference may lead to confused identities or poor policy decisions based on a false sense of what a college or university is and what it has to offer. Ultimately, confusion over their identities can deprive individual colleges and universities as well as state higher education systems of the opportunity to be the best that they can be. "By believing themselves to be what they are not . . . institutions fall short of being what they could be" (Lynton and Elman 1987, p. 13).

To minimize the possibility that claims of distinctiveness merely reflect a desire for its existence, it is important to clarify the meaning of institutional distinctiveness. We also need to understand its effects—that is, how being distinctive can serve both as an advantage and a detriment to a college or university, and what impact distinctive institutions can have on educational outcomes.

These and other issues prompted us to search higher education literature as well as literature on organizational culture, planning, and marketing. Our aim has been to decipher the nature and meaning of institutional distinctiveness in American higher education. We also focused on understanding the concept's usefulness for two major groups: (1) leaders and policy makers committed to the survival of a diverse higher education system in which colleges and universities operate with integrity, and (2) higher education researchers interested in organizational culture, innovation, and institutional leadership.

In this section, we examine the concept of institutional distinctiveness as used in higher education literature and develop a definition of distinctiveness. This definition will guide subsequent section discussions of the origins and character of specific distinctive colleges (Section 2), some lures and perils of a quest for institutional distinctiveness (Section 3), and strategic management decisions influencing the likelihood of becoming distinctive (Section 4).

We conclude with recommendations for institutional and system leaders and researchers (Section 5). Throughout, examples of distinctive colleges and universities are cited. Occasionally we mention some institutions only in passing and do not fully explicate their distinctiveness. Our intent is to provide examples from both the public and private non-profit sectors and from all institutional types.

Characteristics of Distinctive Colleges and Universities

Although assertions of institutional distinctiveness have been part of American higher education rhetoric since the founding of Harvard, institutional distinctiveness as a concept has been studied formally only in the past few decades.

Influenced by the management and planning literature dealing with organizational culture, higher education scholars began to examine colleges and universities as organizations manifesting particular cultures, including cultures conducive to distinctiveness and innovation. Martin's study of the institutional character of four universities and four liberal arts colleges was the first book-length treatment of institutional distinctiveness (1969), while Clark's study of three private liberal arts colleges is probably the best known (1970).

Distinctiveness has been most studied in liberal arts colleges (Martin 1984; Rice and Austin 1988; Riesman, Gusfield, and Gamson 1970; Whitehead, Herbst, and Potts 1991). It also has been studied in community colleges (Townsend 1989a; Roueche and Baker 1987).

Others have applied the concept across institutional types (Grant and Riesman 1978; Kuh and Schuh 1991; Kuh, Schuh, Whitt, & Associates 1991; Martin 1969; Pace 1974) or delineated the distinctive characteristics of a particular institutional type, including the university (Trow 1984; Geiger 1986), historically black colleges (Bowles and DeCosta 1971; Butler 1977; Willie and Edmonds 1978), and women's colleges (Smith 1990). This latter stream of literature often reflects a desire to verify the diversity within American higher education.

Useful as they are, none of these works reflects or develops a commonly accepted definition of institutional distinctiveness. The few explicit definitions of institutional distinctiveness usually cite it as a characteristic that differentiates institutions.

Distinctiveness has been viewed as "how . . . [the institution] is set apart from others" (Moseley 1988, p. 2), perhaps because of its curriculum, clientele, or values (Ewell and

Distinctiveness has been viewed as "how . . . [the institution] is set apart from others."

Lisensky 1988). Similarly, a distinctive college or university is "one which has distinguished itself from other institutions carrying out similar functions" (Townsend 1989b, p. 25). Distinctive schools are those that are "unique or outstanding compared to their institutional peers" (Butler 1977, p. 14). The usually unstated assumption is that colleges and universities are "set apart" or "distinguished" or "unique or outstanding" for positive rather than negative reasons (Townsend 1989b).

Not all agree that institutional distinctiveness is dependent upon comparison to other institutions. Instead, institutional distinctiveness may depend "on internal factors—those, unique, innate elements of institutional life that exist independently of comparison" (Chamberlain 1985, p. 14). Chamberlain identifies eight factors or dimensions of which the interplay contributes to a school's distinctiveness. These dimensions are (1) moral, (2) intellectual, (3) egalitarian, (4) spiritual, (5) socio-political, (6) humane, (7) personal, and (8) tradition.

Institutional members can be surveyed for their perceptions of each dimension's extent and importance within the institution. A composite of individual responses yields "a distinctive profile of that institution" (p. 14). Knowing how internal constituents (faculty, staff, administrators, and students) perceive the college or university's culture can help its leaders make decisions that deliberately will strengthen or diminish these perceptions.

Linking institutional distinctiveness with institutional values and climates, two components of organizational culture, is a common theme in literature addressing institutional distinctiveness in higher education (Birnbaum 1983; Clark 1970; Kuh, Schuh, Whitt, and Associates 1991; Kuh and Schuh 1991; Kuh and Whitt 1988; Laramee 1987; Martin 1969, 1982, 1984; Rice and Austin 1988; Tierney 1988).

Distinctive institutions are viewed as having value systems that have significantly shaped and continue to shape individual and institutional behavior. Motivated by a particular educational vision, a distinctive college harbors a common set of values, norms, and behaviors which help infuse the institution with "a character of its own" (Morgan and Newell 1981, p. 33) or a "strong institutional personality" (Hesburgh 1983, p. 17). Birnbaum has stated this perspective well:

[A] college or university's constituencies may have such unusual values that they manifest themselves in a campus climate sufficiently different from that of other colleges or universities that this difference is noticeable to those outside the institution. Such institutions may be said to be distinctive colleges or universities. Their distinctiveness increases institutional diversity in that they are markedly different institutions from all others on the dimension of values and climate (1983, p. 53).

The likelihood that most colleges and universities can be distinctive nationally in this way is slight (Birnbaum 1983). For example, Bunker Hill Community College values cultural diversity and individuals' ability to adapt to other cultures. The college manifests these values by offering its students and faculty the opportunity to participate in exchange programs with institutions in England and France and in study-travel programs. The college also participates in a special scholarship program that brings Central American students to the campus (Hankin 1989).

Thus, Bunker Hill's commitment to certain values is played out in its curricular and co-curricular activities. However, the college is far from alone in valuing cultural diversity and adaptive abilities. Many two-year as well as four-year colleges hold these values. Bunker Hill would have to hold far more striking values to be considered nationally distinctive.

While a national reputation as a distinctive institution is not possible for most colleges and universities, some well may achieve a degree of distinctiveness through commitment to shared values. Talladega College is one such institution. Founded in 1867 as the first Alabama college for freed slaves, Talladega is committed to a liberal arts education for blacks. In the 1930s its dean, who had been influenced by Robert Hutchins's ideas about general education and by the University of Chicago's embodiment of these ideas, proposed a general education program for Talladega. Offering the B.A. degree only, Talladega encourages its students not only to aim for professions rather than for vocations but also to be conscious of their social responsibility, especially toward blacks.

Many of Talladega's graduates attend graduate and professional schools; upon graduation, many become part of the educated black middle class. While "[t]here is apparently nothing special about the curriculum or even about the teaching at Talladega," what is special is "the quality of daily life at the school, which is suffused with the example of the black struggle, its dignity, and its capacity to 'go beyond'" (Gamson and Associates 1984, p. 74).

Several small, private, liberal arts colleges that share a particular vision of higher education also illustrate how a coherent vision and value structure can guide institutional activities. Committed to the value of a liberal arts education and also valuing community service, Alice Lloyd College, Berea College, Blackburn College, Warren Wilson College, and the School of the Ozarks share a tradition of requiring their students to work—usually on campus—in lieu of paying tuition (except at Warren Wilson) (Greene 1987). Aiming for the "union of head and hand" (Smith 1982, p. 37), this approach "fosters an egalitarian spirit on the campus" (Biemiller 1985, p. 5) which it is hoped will stay with students after they graduate, demonstrating itself in commitment to public service (Greene 1987).

Warren Wilson College is typical of these institutions. It began its 96-year history as the Asheville Farm School founded by the Presbyterian Woman's Board of Home Missions to educate poor boys in the North Carolina mountains. When it merged in 1942 with two women's schools to become a vocational junior college, it was renamed for the former secretary of Rural Church Work for the Presbyterian church's Board of National Missions.

By 1969, the institution no longer was church-affiliated and had become a four-year college. Throughout its existence, Warren Wilson College has maintained a commitment to service through work. Working three hours a day at such tasks as raising the vegetables served at mealtimes and tending the college's cattle and pigs, Warren Wilson students learned to respect manual labor, developed a sense of responsibility for the community, and received the financial benefit of free room and board (Biemiller 1985).

Private liberal arts colleges such as these seem especially suited to the development of a unifying theme, ideology, or value system partly because of their small size. Many liberal arts colleges are relatively small institutions with 2,500 or fewer students (Breneman 1990). For example, Warren Wilson had 573 students in 1991-92, and Talladega enrolled 615 students in 1991-92 (Dilts 1991). Institutions with a small number of faculty and students are better able than large institutions to develop and maintain a distinctive culture (Grant and Associates 1979; Rice and Austin 1988; Kuh and Whitt 1988; Martin 1969; Watts 1972).

Although development of an institutional culture supportive of a unifying theme is most likely to occur in a small, liberal arts college, other institutional types and large colleges and universities also can develop a unifying vision leading to distinctiveness. As an example, the University of Chicago is distinctive even among other research universities for its emphasis on research: "It is the research university's research university" (Heller 1992, p. A18). Functioning as a "community of scholars," the university believes in "learning for its own sake" (p. A18). By limiting its focus to excellence in research and the love of learning, the University of Chicago stands out from the multi-purpose research universities committed to providing something for everyone.

Brooklyn College, a comprehensive college established in 1930 as part of the City University of New York (CUNY) system, is another large school that has been distinctive throughout much of its existence. As one of the CUNY institutions, Brooklyn College initially was perceived as "a poor man's Harvard" and was dedicated to providing a liberal arts education to academically talented commuter students (Hess 1985, p. 263).

In the late 1950s, Brooklyn College was labeled "distinctive" for several reasons. It offered a "free" (no tuition) education to an academically talented, primarily Jewish student body unusually large for a liberal arts college (approximately 17,000 students at the time). Also, to accommodate all these students, Brooklyn College had "possibly the most overworked physical plant in the country"; classes were held from dawn to dusk, an atypical situation in the late 1950s (Boroff 1961, pp. 83-4).

Its tradition of "providing a first-rate education for first-rate students" (p. 103) declined when CUNY established an open enrollment policy in 1969. Brooklyn College's enrollment jumped drastically to almost 35,000 in 1975. With the end of open admissions in 1978, the college reinstated moderately selective admissions standards that contributed to a serious downsizing in enrollment.

Motivated by financial exigency and by the arrival of a new president, Robert L. Hess, institutional members undertook a massive curricular revision so that Brooklyn College again would serve its traditional purpose of providing all students with a rigorous education containing a core curricular experience based in the liberal arts.

Since 1981, all students must take a core curriculum consisting of two five-course tiers. Entrance into the first tier of courses requires passing of standardized examinations in reading, writing, and math; entrance into the second tier requires completion of the first. All the courses were created for the core and "offer both a contemporary perspective and a solid liberal arts base" (Hess 1985). Working with a student body in 1991-92 of 16,042 students, more than 40 percent of whom are minority (Dilts 1991), Brooklyn College has developed a distinctive curriculum that has been widely acknowledged for the quality of its liberal arts experience (e.g., Bennett 1984).

Institutional distinctiveness commonly has been associated with highly selective colleges as in Clark's (1970) use of highly selective Reed, Antioch, and Swarthmore as examples of distinctive colleges. However, excellence in achieving institutional purpose is also a hallmark of distinctive colleges and universities (Pace 1974).

Although institutional excellence perhaps has been the educational cliche of the 1980s, it must be emphasized that distinctive colleges and universities outshine other institutions partly by identifying what they want to do and by doing it well. Sometimes this excellence manifests itself in the form of high admissions standards, but selectivity is not a prerequisite to distinctiveness. Quality in performance is a prerequisite. By this equation, a non-selective college or university can achieve distinctiveness if it achieves its desired goals.

Alverno College provides an example of one such school. Created from institutions which had a purpose to prepare Sisters of Saint Francis for the traditional female vocations of teaching, nursing, and music, Alverno lost its primary reason for existence when the order decided to require its future entrants to hold a college degree. Prompted by declining enrollments, shaky finances, and feminist questions about the relevance of the curriculum to women's lives, its leaders began a reexamination which would "question . . . [Alverno's] very identity as an institution of higher learning for women" (Read and Sharkey 1985, p. 197).

The result was a commitment to Alverno as a "community of learning" (p. 196) valuing teaching, communal involvement in curricular and organizational development, and research-based innovation. Major changes were made in the curriculum by incorporating a competence-based approach to education in its curriculum. This commitment to education for competence reflected the sisters' wish that they had been educated for "worldly competence" (Grant and Associates 1979). Alverno faculty and administrators have developed eight explicit outcomes or competencies for the institution's 35 programs. To graduate, students must demonstrate achievement in each of the competencies.

Alverno also has developed an assessment model which measures students individually in relation to their initial performance in each competency. The assessment, which takes a variety of forms, is conducted by both internal and external assessors. Widely praised as a pioneer in the student assessment movement (Magner 1989), in 1991-92 Alverno enrolled 2,414 students with average ACT scores over 21 (Dilts 1991).

Alverno College's distinctiveness, achieved through its competency-based education and assessment of individual students, developed partly through a commitment to reforming education and partly through a desire to ensure survival (Grant and Associates 1979; Read and Sharkey 1985). In the process of developing a distinctive approach to education, Alverno has increased its institutional status, winning acclaim as a regional liberal arts college (*America's Best Colleges 1991*).

In sum, from prior writings about institutional distinctiveness we can glean several characteristics often attributed to distinctive colleges and universities. First, their organizational cultures embody commitment to a particular educational vision or theme. This vision or theme represents institutional values manifested in programs, services, and other activities.

Second, distinctive schools are committed to excellence in achieving a clearly defined purpose. Although one manifestation of this excellence may be upholding very high admission standards, an academically elite student body is not essential for institutional distinctiveness. Witness Alverno College. Additionally, large size is not a barrier to distinctiveness. Although distinctive institutions are often small, private, liberal arts colleges, large, public, comprehensive colleges or universities also can be distinctive through commitment to a unifying theme embodying shared institutional values.

Toward a Definition of Institutional Distinctiveness

Shared institutional values are essential to institutional distinctiveness. Drawing from some of the literature about organizations in general, we shall show how internal as well as external constituents must be aware of these values for an institution to be considered distinctive. We also maintain that for a distinctive college or university to be successful in the marketplace, external constituents must not only be aware of these values—but also value them.

Every organization has an image that "consist[s] not only of images of 'fact' but also images of 'value'" (Boulding 1961, p. 11). Its factual images are the organization's empirical reality—what the organization is and does. Its images of value reflect how internal and external observers rate its factual images in comparison to images of other institutions. For example, among its several images, Harvard University has the factual image of being a highly selective university. In viewing Harvard, individuals perceive this factual image and rate it in comparison to the same factual image of other universities. Additionally, images of value also reflect the extent to which observers value or esteem the factual images.

Because images of value are dependent upon comparison to other institutions, those within a school may view it as very distinctive, even though external constituencies do not (Leister and Maclachlan 1975). Only when external constituencies such as legislators, potential donors, and potential students see a college or university's images of fact and view them as special in comparison to other institution's factual images is an institution truly distinctive. Ultimately, the degree of acceptance a distinctive college or university finds in the marketplace depends on how much its factual images are also images of value for external constituents.

To recapitulate, *institutional distinctiveness is a phenomenon resulting from a common set of values that shape institutional activities and unite key constituencies, both internal and external.* A distinctive college or university has a unifying set of values that are apparent to and esteemed by faculty, students, staff, alumni, and the public.

A college may enroll one type of student such as women, men, or people with disabilities. Merely admitting a specific type of student does not qualify a school as distinctive, merely as different. A distinctive college or university would admit only students of a particular type, because limiting the student body in this way is a reflection of certain institutional values and of a particular approach to education. From this perspective, a women's college that does not consider the gender of its student body in curricular decisions contributes to institutional diversity, but not to distinctiveness.

Gallaudet University and Landmark College provide extreme examples of institutions that are distinctive because of their commitment to a particular educational approach with a very specific student constituency. Gallaudet is the only American higher education institution designed exclusively for deaf and hearing-impaired students. From its inception in 1864 as the National Deaf Mute College, it has been committed to providing collegiate-level instruction in the liberal arts and sciences to a segment of the population not normally sought out by colleges and universities. Currently offering more than 45 majors to over 1,900 undergraduate and graduate students ("On the Green" 1989-90), Gallaudet uses a specific teaching-learning process. Instead of using interpreters, both teachers and students use American Sign Language simultaneously with speech or mouth movement (*Gallaudet University* n.d.).

Like Gallaudet, Landmark College is also a distinctive institution that was created from a desire to serve a very specific and neglected constituency—individuals with dyslexia or certain learning disabilities (Meyer 1986, p. 2). A two-year college established in 1985, it is the only college in the world specifically developed for these students.

In its program, Landmark eschews such standard academic strategies for dyslexic students as having others take notes for the students or permitting them to take oral exams. Instead, students undergo a highly structured liberal arts program requiring them to live on an alcohol- and drug-free campus, attend classes every day from 8 a.m. to 3:30 p.m., and study during residency hall quiet hours. In such an environment students learn the basic communication skills necessary for success in any standard academic environment (*Landmark College Catalogue 1989-91* 1989; Wald 1986). It is Landmark College's restriction of admission to students with learning disorders combined with its educational approach toward dyslexic students and others with related learning disorders that makes the college distinctive.

Finally, it is important to note that for most colleges and universities, distinctiveness is a phenomenon that develops slowly over time as the institution incorporates certain values and manifests them in its activities. Recall that Alverno College had roots stretching back to the late 19th century but did not become nationally prominent until the 1970s and 1980s. It took time for Alverno to develop a vision of itself and of education which was sufficiently distinctive to merit national recognition. Gallaudet and Landmark were distinctive from their inception, but most colleges and universities do not begin as nationally distinctive. Those that do may not long endure as is recounted in sections 2 and 3. Thus we note the aspect of temporality in our definition of distinctiveness.

Summary

Distinctive colleges and universities exhibit certain characteristics: commitment to a unifying theme representative of generally held institutional values, the integrity to exclude activities inconsistent with institutional values, and excellence in achieving their overall purpose. Frequently, distinctive schools are small, liberal arts colleges with a highly selective student body, but neither small size nor an academically talented student body are prerequisites to distinctiveness.

The link between institutional distinctiveness and organizational culture, as manifested in a college or university's values, may be the source of the usually implied connection between distinctiveness and excellence or high quality. While high quality is partly a measure of quantifiable factors such as the ability level of the student body or the scholarly activity of faculty, the quality also seems to be a reflection of a college or university's organizational culture. Certain institutions have cultures which embody and reflect values and beliefs and assumptions conducive to high quality. Colleges and universities with such an organizational culture emerge as distinctive from other institutions within the same type. Additionally, those who espouse examining the values of a school tend to hold up for praise those colleges or universities that have cultures supportive of excellence in the two most commonly stated functions of higher education institutions—namely, the teaching-learning process and research.

The role of values plays an important part in our definition of institutional distinctiveness. We argue that institutional distinctiveness is usually a slowly emerging phenomenon that develops as institutional activities increasingly reflect educational values strongly held by senior administrators and faculty. This distinctiveness is maintained if sufficient external constituencies also share these values and perceive the college or university to hold them clearly in comparison to other colleges and universities.

AIMS AND IDEAS: TEN DISTINCTIVE COLLEGES AND THEIR LEGACIES

Distinctive colleges strengthen higher education in the same fashion that biodiversity serves the natural world. They foster practices and harbor ideas that are essential to the vitality and responsiveness of undergraduate programs everywhere. While distinctive colleges are vastly outnumbered by their less adventurous sibling institutions, they are a font of diverse thought, a stimulus to question prevailing assumptions, and, sometimes, a source of inspiration and courage.

Rhythms of Birthing and Ironies of Fate

Distinctive colleges and universities often emerge by responding to crises in the social order or by anticipating cultural or demographic trends. Changes in the production and organization of knowledge, like those that came with the spread of German-style universities in America at the turn of the century, also can precipitate experimentation with new structures and curricular forms in undergraduate education. Further, traditional institutions, when faced with stagnation or decline, occasionally transform themselves by pursuing an imaginative new vision.

Whatever their origins, truly distinctive schools remind us that significant educational innovations are possible and that bold reforms often can be sustained. The best of these maverick institutions keep affirming their experimental heritages by continuing to exercise and develop alternatives to conventional educational practices.

A break with tradition is never simple. Distinctive colleges and universities are not easily launched, relaunched, or kept under sail. New schools with distinctive philosophies most frequently are founded when existing institutions fall noticeably short of meeting societal, community, or individual needs. The wider the gap between need and response, the more likely knowledgeable and creative people will muster the resources and find the courage to start something new. It is natural, then, that many of America's most successful uncommon colleges and universities trace their origins to periods of intense social upheaval or educational ferment. The mortality among these daring institutions also runs high, as we will see, especially in their early years.

We now turn our attention to ten colleges that are (or once were) simultaneously different in character and excellent in quality. In its heyday, at least, each of these institutions exhibited three characteristics: (1) it had a distinct educational philosophy, (2) it inspired commitment to that philosophy among faculty, students, staff, and alumni, and (3) it created instructional practices consistent with its educational values. Our purpose is to explore *why* and *how* these colleges came into existence and to see how their ideas worked out, not to write their histories or fully describe their programs.

With these aims in mind, we will probe the ideas, motives, and leaders who gave life to ten unusual American colleges. A web of *connections* and *tensions* among the reformers and their philosophies will become increasingly evident as we proceed.

Striving to Create a New Moral Order

Two of the oldest distinctive colleges in the United States, Antioch and Berea, came to life when the federal union was torn by the elemental moral and economic struggles that led to the Civil War. This mid-19th century malaise in American life arose from the unrealized promise of the Jeffersonian and Jacksonian visions of democracy and from unresolvable conflicts among citizens over the practice of slavery.

Horace Mann spoke to both issues. A former member of Congress and continuing abolitionist crusader, he was also an educational reformer of the first order. A champion of universal public instruction, he invested much of his life in efforts to reorient and restructure public education.

In the early 1850s, Mann shifted his focus to the reform of higher education and became the founding president of **Antioch College** in southwestern Ohio (Clark 1970). The growth and promise of the Ohio and Mississippi valleys convinced Mann of the need for a college equal to the challenge of creating a truly democratic society in the American West.

Thousands of people flocked to pastoral Yellow Springs to see the imposing four-story, eight-spired edifice of Antioch Hall and hear Horace Mann's 1853 inaugural address. Antioch College, he told the crowd, must devote itself to nurturing democratic principles and to building "the Glory of God and the service of men" (Morgan 1938, p. 187). Foreshadowing a 20th-century cliche, he expressed the hope that Antioch might become "a little Harvard of the West" (Henderson and Hall 1946).

At Antioch's 1859 commencement, shortly before his death, Mann delivered the supreme charge to a graduating class: "I beseech you to treasure up in your hearts these my final words: Be ashamed to die until you have won some victory for humanity" (Morgan 1938, p. 389). Mann's college had a mission and it was related to a new vision of American democracy rather than the preservation of a socio-economic elite. Far ahead of its time, Antioch admitted academically qualified students without regard to their race, gender, religion, or family wealth.

Encouraging interactive teaching methods instead of traditional recitation, Mann hoped that Antioch would set the students' "minds free from prejudice and yearning for truth" (*Antioch Catalog* 1990-91). Oberlin College, Antioch's Ohio neighbor to the north, initiated co-education in 1837, but Antioch pioneered an even broader progressive mission. In defense of his commitment to gender equity, Mann noted that "female education should be rescued from its present reproach of inferiority" (Morgan 1938, p. 256).

If Antioch began with a grand vision, it also struggled for many years with meager results. Shortly before he died, Mann posted a sizable portion of his own assets to rescue the school from bankruptcy. The college survived, but it graduated only about five students per year until well after the turn of the century.

Antioch College was on the ropes in 1920 when another educational visionary, Arthur Morgan, presented a daring plan to save the college. The board accepted his plan and promptly appointed Morgan president (Clark 1970). A vigorous 42-year-old engineer, he believed a college education should be a complete experience involving the integration of liberal arts study with practical work, democratic participation with community service, and personal commitment with social responsibility. He built on Mann's idealism, reached beyond it, and made the plan work.

Under Arthur Morgan, Antioch experienced a new dawn of purpose and confidence, becoming a pioneering institution in cooperative work-study programs and student participation in academic and community governance. Morgan's new mission for Antioch was consistent with, but extended beyond, the historic aims of the college.

Antioch has continued to innovate, but not without trauma. It reached beyond its limits in the 1960s and 1970s, spawning new centers across the United States and then consolidating them as Antioch University. Once again, in the mid-1980s,

Mann's college had a mission and it was related to a new vision of American democracy rather than the preservation of a socio-economic elite.

a new president and an awakened board teamed up to steady the institution, trim its sails, and assure its survival among the nation's distinctive liberal arts colleges. Antioch College, at the original Yellow Springs site, remains the hub of the pruned, but scattered, university network.

Two contemporaries of Horace Mann in the 1850s, the Reverend John G. Fee and Cassius M. Clay, also felt inspired to found a school equal to the challenges of their time and place. Fee was an abolitionist pastor educated in Cincinnati. Clay, a gentleman farmer, was also repulsed by slavery and dreamed of creating a utopian agricultural community in which human dignity might be blossom. Together they opened a Kentucky school in 1855, formally chartered as **Berea College** in 1859. Its aims were to advance Christian principles, provide education for young men and women of high moral character, offer meaningful work for all students, and keep tuition costs low (Hutchins 1963; Peck 1982).

Berea intended to throw its doors open to students throughout the region—male and female, black and white, orthodox and unorthodox. Inspired by religious idealism but unrestrained by religious doctrines, it aimed to offer educational opportunities to students with the hope that they would return or proceed to Appalachian communities, both enlightened and prepared to lift others. It was a bold start.

Neighbors along Berea Ridge took little note of this radical educational experiment, until John Brown's raid at Harpers Ferry ignited widespread paranoia. Rumors that abolitionist Fee just might instigate similar acts in Kentucky resulted in demands for his departure—backed by a show of arms. Fee and several key members of the faculty retreated to Cincinnati in January 1860. Berea suspended classes indefinitely (Hutchins 1963).

Reverend Fee and his colleagues returned to reopen Berea College after the Civil War, beginning anew with 96 black and 91 white students. President Henry Fairchild and his successors eventually developed a labor program in which students have done everything from constructing campus buildings and running the town fire department to vegetable farming and woodworking (fine woodcrafts would become a Berea trademark).

Until the 1890s, Berea sought students from north and south alike. But under the leadership of President William G. Frost, the college began to redefine its mission to serve—

especially the higher education aspirations of deserving students in the mountain region around it. In 1915, the trustees restricted admissions almost exclusively to Appalachian students. The school has continued to concentrate on educating first-generation college students from this area (Peck 1982).

A major challenge to Berea College arose when the 1904 Kentucky legislature passed a law that prohibited educating blacks and whites together. Berea persistently contested this discriminatory law—finally in a U.S. Supreme Court case—but did not prevail. The college was forced to stop admitting black students until the Civil Rights movement induced changes in federal policy and Kentucky law at mid-century (Smith 1950). Berea moved quickly to make up lost opportunities. However, newly affirmative admissions policies at other colleges in recent years have posed difficulties for Berea in regaining its previous high proportion of black students.

Antioch College and Berea College were founded by leaders impelled to action by a sense of moral duty and even outrage, coupled with a personal determination to act. These colleges represented responses to their times and were products of the ethical will of their founders. Both schools have been revitalized at least once by subsequent visionary leaders. Each has survived and now thrives despite the rough seas it has negotiated over a century and a half.

Progressive Zeal in a New Century

The progressive movement in American politics, which focused on the reform of our major public and private institutions including education, produced a number of experimental colleges in the first two decades of the 20th century. Two that continue to flourish are Reed College in Portland, Ore., and Deep Springs College near Bishop, Calif. The founders of both schools were beneficiaries of America's burgeoning industrial economy, and each sought to create a college tailored to the challenges of a new period in history. In this era, business was king, the American West was open, and new forms of higher education were in the making.

Reed College opened its doors in 1911, thanks to the estate of a land and mine developer, Simeon Gannett Reed, whose widow, Amanda, provided the funds. A Unitarian pastor, Thomas Lamb Eliot, whose father had founded Washington University in St. Louis in the 1860s, proffered the idea and plan. To serve the educational and cultural needs of fledgling

Portland, Eliot aimed to create an elite learning community capable of attracting the best students, inspiring them with a love of knowledge and culture, and motivating them to enrich their society (Clark 1970; Ritz 1990).

From the beginning, Reed's students were challenged to meet high academic standards in an environment spared of fraternities and intercollegiate athletics. Small classes and discussions, rather than lectures, became the common mode of learning. Grades were deemphasized, and the liberal arts provided the spirit and structure of education (Clark 1970; Martines 1985).

On the spectrum from intellectual to "whole person" education, Reed continues to hover near the middle. Its aims and traditions are avowedly intellectual—stressing particularly critical thinking and lofty academic standards—but Reed expects students to participate in campus governance, voluntary service projects, and summer internships. The curriculum combines a common year-long interdisciplinary course on the foundations of western civilization with gradually increasing opportunities for independent study. Much of the teaching is tutorial. In their final year, students are provided individual work stations to pursue a research project or creative activity and write a senior thesis (Clark 1970; Reed Catalog 1990).

Reed College takes a philosophical middle ground between a structured great books curriculum and a self-designed elective course of study. It poises its program between pure contemplative study and specialized investigation of contemporary issues. For a college with a long history of nonconformist educational aims and methods, Reed is distinguished for its refusal to regard competing instructional philosophies as mutually exclusive notions. Reed College remains a highly respected, high-tuition, four-year school that enrolls about 1,300 students.

Another western industrialist and miner, L.L. Nunn, invested his fortune and declining years in the creation of Deep Springs College (Newell 1982; Breiseth 1983). A restless bachelor and successful entrepreneur, Nunn believed America's future depended on the preparation of able and visionary leaders dedicated to the well-being of their society.

From the outset, Nunn sought to remove his students from the superficialities of ordinary campus social life, so that they could think and work without distraction. To do this, he bought a remote cattle ranch in Inyo County, Calif., in the evening shadow of the Sierra Nevada range, constructed a few academic buildings, and in 1917 opened Deep Springs.

Believing, like Thomas Jefferson, that talent is dispersed throughout society with little regard for station or wealth, Nunn founded what might best be described as an honors junior college. Deep Springs' students are admitted solely on the basis of promise for leadership—as best this quality can be judged. "Deep Springers" are recruited nationally and internationally, and they study without cost.

However, students are expected to dedicate their lives thereafter to the common good—however they choose to define it. This bond is known as the ethic of Deep Springs— what it means to prepare for and live "a life of service" is a matter of enduring reflection and debate at the college.

Nunn set out to educate "the whole man," but only a few at a time. For 75 years, Deep Springs has enrolled about twenty- four students, employed a faculty of six, and offered a multifaceted liberal education experience. Under the supervision of a ranch manager and a farmer, Deep Springs' academically gifted students, all male to this day, are expected to provide all the labor and make many of the decisions necessary to sustain the community—from working the ranch and milking the cows to managing the library and electing their own labor commissioner. They do this, while also pursuing a demanding academic program and participating fully in governing the school. In 1917, Nunn specified that an elected student representative would serve as a voting member of the board of trustees. No college in American history has so fully delegated responsibility to its students.

Deep Springs offers a liberal education curriculum that emphasizes study of the human heritage, relationships between the individual and community, and courses tailored to the school's high desert setting—often astronomy, geology, ecology, and zoology. The only required course is public speaking. The founder believed knowledge is distorted or wasted unless clearly communicated. Deep Springers typically transfer to the nation's leading universities to complete their studies. Nearly 60 percent of the alumni hold doctoral degrees, and many have pursued careers in public service (Newell 1982).

Deep Springs celebrated its 75th anniversary in 1992, having seldom passed a placid year. The intensity of an isolated community of high-achieving people (faculty, staff, and students), the precariousness of a ranching operation on the desert, and the uncommonly participatory governance structure, combine to produce almost perpetual turbulence and, often, intense loyalty. For all this, Deep Springs has as long and steady a record of fidelity to its founder's innovative aims and design as any distinctive college in America.

The Battle of Progressives and Neo-Classicists In The Thirties

The progressive movement in education produced a wealth of ideas and counter-ideas about higher education in the late 1920s and 1930s. In this era, the stimulus for creating distinctive colleges arose primarily from strains *within* academe itself.

It was now more than half a century since Johns Hopkins University opened its doors, and many other universities had since adopted the German pattern—based on professorial specialization, departmental organization, and research orchestration. The benefits of university research for America's industrial and military establishments were already evident— as were the implications of this new organizational structure for undergraduate teaching.

The controversy over the relationship between research and teaching, which continues to dog us, called forth a pantheon of reformers. Their philosophies reflected a common interest in the future of American democracy and the place of higher education in serving it, but their prescriptions often differed as sharply as their personalities.

John Dewey championed a problem-centered and relatively free educational environment for the preparation of citizens in a democratic society (Meiklejohn 1945). Alexander Meiklejohn believed that if education was to enhance "intelligence capable of being applied to any field whatever," it must be both carefully structured and intellectually searching, especially for lower division students (Meiklejohn 1932, p. 13). Dewey and Meiklejohn had their differences, particularly over the importance of structuring educational content and learning activities (Cadwallader 1984).

If Dewey championed freedom and discovery in learning and self-discipline in education, another crusading reformer of undergraduate education, Robert Maynard Hutchins, was going another way. When Hutchins assumed the presidency of the University of Chicago, his dream was to create within this institution a strong and independent undergraduate college. Fearing that great ideas were being swamped in a sea of technical information, Hutchins based his plan on the study of classic works—on the major ideas that underpin western civilization (Cadwallader 1984).

Around 1930, Alexander Meiklejohn, Robert Hutchins, and others invested their energies and lives in creating experimental colleges *within* great research universities—rather than in founding new liberal arts colleges. If universities begat the problems, then universities are where solutions should be invented and tested. For this era, we will look especially at Hutchins' Chicago College Plan, known best as "the College," and at Meiklejohn's Experimental College at the University of Wisconsin. But we also will consider two other legacies of this era, both of them independent colleges that owe their inspiration to the university reformers: Black Mountain College in North Carolina and the rebirth of St. John's College in Maryland.

Reflecting, no doubt, the influence of Robert LaFollette and the progressive tradition in Wisconsin politics, the University of Wisconsin was at its apogee in the 1930s. It was a wild and exciting place, comparable to the University of California at Berkeley several decades later. Alexander Meiklejohn landed and took root in this loosened soil in 1926.

The controversial former president of Amherst College, a philosopher and restless reformer, Meiklejohn gained presidential support to establish an experimental lower-division college within the University of Wisconsin. He and his faculty colleagues hammered out a set of principles to guide teaching and curriculum development in the college and introduced the program the fall of 1927.

The curriculum at the **Experimental College at the University of Wisconsin** was a single integrated course of study that lasted throughout students' freshman and sophomore years. There were no electives nor any majors. Everything focused on the nature and functions of human societies. Students' first year was devoted to the study of fifth-century Athens and the second to examining contemporary American life. Segments within the course dealt with such topics as social structure, government, economics, literature, philosophy, and the arts.

Students received no formal evaluations of the quality of their academic work until the end of the second year when an oral examination required them to summarize and apply what they had learned. In 1928, Meiklejohn and his colleagues added a third element to the curriculum, "regional study," in which each student conducted a thorough examination of a specific American community—preferably his or her home town (Meiklejohn 1932; Cadwallader 1984; Tussman 1984).

Meiklejohn's Experimental College was a bold effort and a controversial one. It inspired phenomenal loyalty and dedication among its students and faculty, but the university's faculty senate withdrew its support and the college collapsed in 1932. Meiklejohn bravely moved on to teach at Berkeley, but his students had formed bonds with each other—and with him—that endured for decades. He continued to teach and write about his ideas until he died at the age of 93.

Now, 60 years after the college closed, surviving alumni continue their association with one another and with Meiklejohn's legacy (Tussman 1984). No single experiment in American higher education has been more written about or more emulated than Meiklejohn's educational shooting star at the University of Wisconsin.

Robert Maynard Hutchins had just passed his 30th birthday when the University of Chicago inaugurated him its fifth president in 1929. He had previously served as dean and professor of law at Yale. Influenced by the veteran president of Berea College (who happened to be his father) and by his senior colleague and mentor, Alexander Meiklejohn, Hutchins possessed both an indomitable will and a passion to reform undergraduate education at Chicago. Disgusted by college curricula and pedagogies tailored particularly to advance scientific and technical learning as well as by increasingly specialized instruction in the arts and humanities, Hutchins had a clear idea of what might be—and ample energy and courage to pursue his dreams (Hutchins 1934).

Among American academic leaders, Clark Kerr believes that Hutchins was one of "the last of the university presidents who really tried to change his institution and higher education in a fundamental way" (Kerr 1982, p. 33).

Lamenting the demise of the classical curriculum and determined to diminish the influence of the departmental system on undergraduate teaching, Hutchins threw down the gauntlet in his inaugural address. The University of Chicago, he said, ". . . cannot pile course on course. It must set up clear and

comprehensible goals for its students to reach. It must articulate its courses, squeezing out waste, water, and duplication.
It cannot tolerate education by the adding machine. . ." The
new president continued, ". . . the college that wishes to solve
the problem of how to develop and how to administer a liberal education must have a faculty devoted to this task" (Ward
1950, p. 39).

Influenced by Meiklejohn, Hutchins proposed revamping
the freshman and sophomore courses of study to provide a
sturdy intellectual base to underpin specialized study at higher
levels. As president, Hutchins also encouraged and supported
innovative teaching, placement tests for advising students,
and the publication of course syllabi with complete bibliog-
raphies and sample examinations. His plans eventually
included jurisdiction over the final two years of the University
High School that had been established by John Dewey. Setting
forth his ideas in *The Higher Learning in America* (1936),
Hutchins advocated "a course of study consisting of the great
books of the western World and the arts of reading, writing,
thinking, and speaking together with mathematics. . ." (Ward
1950, p. 57). The refinement of "human reason" was his goal.

The wheels of reform ground slowly at Chicago. Year by
year for more than a decade the program took shape, but it
wasn't until 1942 that the faculty senate finally granted "the
College" full status as an independent entity, free of departmental control. In its bloom, the **College of the University
of Chicago** set its own academic policies, offered an integrated and highly structured four-year curriculum, and
awarded bachelor's degrees after successful completion of
a comprehensive examination. Students did not pursue a disciplinary major.

Hutchins' Chicago plan differed significantly from Meiklejohn's Experimental College at Wisconsin because it applied
to *all* undergraduate students, not just to a small subgroup
who opted for it. In this sense, Hutchins' college was a much
more ambitious undertaking and took much longer to build—
and a little longer to run its course—than the Experimental
College.

When Robert Hutchins moved on to the Ford Foundation
in 1951, the College quickly lost its character and indepen-
dence. Without Hutchins' presence to help suppress them,
old faculty jealousies and wounds resurfaced and departments
quickly reasserted influence over the College. Vestiges of the

core curriculum persist, as does the liberal education emphasis in the undergraduate curriculum, but disciplinary majors have since flowered at Chicago as well.

Black Mountain College is an entirely different story. It wasn't planned, nor did it spring from a clearly articulated vision of what might be. It just happened. John Andrew Rice got his walking papers from Rollins College in Florida for arrogant and audacious behavior, claimed by the president to be "disruptive of peace and harmony" on the campus (Duberman 1972, p. 19). A professor of ancient languages, he often shocked his students—or at least the administration—by espousing his radical social theories. It was 1933 and the Great Depression was at its depth. Rice's firing, precipitated by his outspoken opposition to the president's pet curriculum proposal, divided the faculty, called forth an academic freedom investigation by the American Association of University Professors (AAUP), and inadvertently launched Rice on a new venture.

Goaded by other Rollins College dissidents, Rice toyed with the idea of starting a college based on his own educational ideas. With a financial assist from the wealthy Forbes family of Massachusetts, and academic counsel from brother-in-law Frank Aydolette (Swarthmore's inventive president), Rice rented the Black Mountain Assembly's old summer camp in North Carolina's Blue Ridge Mountains. Classes opened that autumn with nearly as many faculty as students. The entire community numbered only three dozen souls.

Black Mountain started with a meager liberal arts curriculum based simply on the competence of the faculty who opted to join Rice there. Paid only a pittance, they traded security for freedom. Classes were informal and interactive, but students were expected to prepare rigorously and participate actively. A loosely organized farm labor program took a stab at self-sufficiency and, for a time, provided tuition waivers for needy students. But this arrangement smacked of the caste system, and farm labor soon became a general responsibility—and eventually, no one's responsibility (Adamic 1938; Duberman 1972; Lane 1990).

An admirer of John Dewey, whom he enticed to visit Black Mountain occasionally, Rice sparred publicly with Chicago's Robert Maynard Hutchins over his single-minded interest in a set curriculum anchored in classical literature. "Why exclude from general education all but one means of getting experience?" Rice asked. "To read a play is good, to see a play is better, but to act in a play, however awkwardly, is to realize a subtle relationship between sound and motion . . ." (Rice 1937, p. 588). From studies in art and architecture to geometry and natural science, creative expressionism became the key to learning (Dawson 1970; Buchanan 1985).

Black Mountain was to become one of the most free-wheeling colleges in American history. Scarred by his unhappy experiences at Rollins College, Rice opposed the appointment of a board of trustees and stuck by his decision. The original faculty worked only for room and board and taught pretty much what they wished. Individual choice was central to Rice's philosophy and to those drawn to him, as was the conviction that learning should engage a student's experience and emotions as much as it does his or her mind.

Tending toward the fine arts from the beginning, Black Mountain moved increasingly in that direction when Josef Albers fled Nazi Germany and came to teach at the college in 1934. Under Albers's influence, experiential education abounded in art workshops, musical productions, plays, and literary readings (Duberman 1972).

Black Mountain caught the public's fancy and became a lightning rod for educational controversy within academe and in the public press. The outspoken Rice, however, neglected college administrative affairs in pursuit of other interests and finally bowed to faculty pressure to resign.

Josef Albers, the Prussian painter, then assumed leadership at Black Mountain. He launched a series of summer institutes in the arts, lost interest in liberal education, overextended the meager budget, and alienated key donors. Deciding to quit after a few stormy years, Albers tried to right the balance sheet by selling part of the pastoral campus to neighboring farmers before he left.

In 1951, Charles Olson, a well-known writer, became rector (chairing the three-member Board of Fellows). But the school continued to disintegrate. From a peak of 90 students in the 1940s, Black Mountain dwindled to about 20 in the early 1950s. In the fall of 1956, Olson announced his disinterest in meeting his classes and quit. So did everyone else. After 23 turbulent years, Black Mountain College expired (Bentley 1945; Duberman 1972; Harris 1987). Surviving alumni gathered for a reunion in San Francisco in 1992, suggesting once more the influence experimental colleges exert.

Black Mountain caught the public's fancy and became a lightning rod for educational controversy within academe and in the public press.

St. John's College began as King William's School in 1696; the name was changed to St. John's after the American revolution. Located in Annapolis, Md., it survived as a traditional, private liberal arts college until the early 1930s. Academic and financial mismanagement brought the college to the brink of oblivion in 1935—when its accreditation was suspended and bankruptcy was in the offing (Tilghman 1984).

Faced with this crisis, the trustees resolved to take an all-or-nothing leap. They turned to two professors—historian Stringfellow Barr and philosopher Scott Buchanan—who had tried unsuccessfully to reform undergraduate education at the University of Virginia. The St. John's trustees appointed Barr president and Buchanan academic dean.

Friends since their student days at Oxford, the two had worked together as members of a presidential commission at Virginia that advocated a Great Books curriculum for the honors program there. Buchanan had studied under the personal direction of Alexander Meiklejohn as an undergraduate at Amherst College, and he later had participated with Robert Maynard Hutchins in his initial efforts to launch the Chicago Plan (Tilghman 1984; Tussman 1984).

Propelled by the risks they had taken in trading secure faculty positions at the University of Virginia for leadership opportunities at a collapsing college, Barr and Buchanan proceeded to revolutionize St. John's. With strong support from the board of trustees and virtually no resistance from a dispirited faculty, they dusted off their University of Virginia honors program proposal and installed it at St. John's. This curriculum probably exceeded the fondest dreams of both Meiklejohn and Hutchins.

St. John's rolled back over a century of change in college curricula by eliminating all electives *and* basing the four-year integrated course of instruction exclusively on reading approximately 100 of the most influential books in western civilization. Students were to encounter great ideas from original texts, not through modern scholars' interpretations and commentaries about these works. The neo-classical curriculum, therefore, included two years of Greek followed by two years of French, so that students could read many of the authors in the original (Brann 1984; Tilghman 1984).

Beginning anew in the fall of 1937 with fewer than 50 students and a half-dozen faculty, St. John's College quickly gained both notoriety and students. It found itself on rather secure footing within a few years. John Dewey, Sydney Hook, and Helen Lynd, among others, assailed St. John's as an unfortunate and elitist throwback to earlier centuries. However, Robert Hutchins, Alexander Meiklejohn, and others came to the defense of Barr and Buchanan's experiment. As so often happens, the controversy itself brought the St. John's College program to the attention of educators throughout America— and attracted students as well (Meiklejohn 1945; Tilghman 1984).

St. John's so prospered that in 1964 it opened a second campus in Santa Fe, N.M. Never enrolling more than about 800 students at its two campuses, St. John's has maintained with integrity the spirit and character or the education envisioned and initiated by Stringfellow Barr and Scott Buchanan (St. John's Catalog 1990-91). "St. Johnnies," as students and alumni refer to themselves, are selected from an intellectual elite and come largely from privileged socio-economic strata (Boroff 1963; Tilghman 1984).

Since its reformation in 1937, St. John's has existed without academic departments, without faculty ranks, without posting students' grades (beyond acceptable or unacceptable), and without apology for its completely structured curriculum and philosophical-historical focus. Faculty are regarded as "tutors," with the real teachers being the authors of the classical texts. "We are not looking for the last word on those subjects," Alexander Meiklejohn said in defense of St. John's College in 1945, "but instead for the first words . . . from the time of the Greeks until the present" (Meiklejohn 1945, p. 108). St. John's makes no pretense of professional training or academic major concentrations. Its aim is to educate students for living, not for employment, and thus assert itself as a "vocational school without a vocation" (J.A. Rice 1942).

Upheavals and Creations: Siren Songs of the Sixties
The 1960s, like the 1930s, saw the founding of a new wave of distinctive colleges. If the practices of the new research universities and the anguish of the great depression had precipitated an earlier reform movement, then the social unrest caused by the Vietnam War and the Civil Rights movement— as well as the continued increases in higher education enrollments—seemed to foster plans for new colleges and innovations in the late 1960s. Two illustrative but contrasting examples include Washington's Evergreen State College and the College of the Atlantic in Maine.

A combination of factors converged in the founding of **Evergreen State College** in Olympia, Wash. In the mid-1960s, the presidents of Washington's five state institutions of higher learning began to talk of founding a sixth institution to serve the southwest region of the state. The legislature bought the idea in 1967 and appointed a board of trustees to plan the new college. They appointed Charles McCann, formerly dean of the faculty at Central Washington State College, as the first president of Evergreen (Jones and Smith 1984). A natural innovator, McCann hired three deans who had extensive experience with interdisciplinary and experimental programs at other colleges and universities. They, in turn, hired 18 faculty members, and the entire group was given a full year to plan the college's initial policies and programs.

The experimental spirit of the 1930s came to bear through the extended influence of Alexander Meiklejohn—who had been a teacher and mentor of Mervyn Cadwallader, one of the founding deans. Cadwallader also had been an associate of Joseph Tussman, whose experimental efforts at Berkeley earlier in the 1960s were well known and whose book *Experiment at Berkeley* (1969) inspired Evergreen's planners. Tussman and Meiklejohn may have captured the imagination of Evergreen's faculty, but only certain elements of their dreams persisted to implementation.

The Evergreen faculty chose to ignore common practices for organizing courses, credits, and faculty in favor of establishing learning groups of students and faculty clustered around ideas of compelling interest or problems of particular urgency to the participants (Jones 1981). Evergreen, then, took a central idea from two failed experiments (Wisconsin from 1927-32 and Berkeley in the 1960s) and made it work in a brand-new college. Where Meiklejohn and Tussman had tried to create experimental colleges *within* established universities, Evergreen faced less resistance and enjoyed greater success by going it alone.

Evergreen State College opened its doors in October 1971 to approximately 1,000 students. Like most experimental colleges, the new school appealed particularly to politically liberal students. Controversial from the start, Evergreen survived its most vulnerable years with the help of progressive governor Dan Evans—who moved to the Evergreen presidency when he left political office. His political savvy and popularity served Evergreen well at a time when many experiments find themselves rather exposed—shortly after they get underway.

Evergreen State College now enrolls roughly 3,500 students, continues to eschew faculty ranks and academic departments, and expects every course to be theme oriented, experiential based, and team taught (Biemiller 1988). It has maintained its philosophical resolve to put tutorial methods of teaching, interdisciplinary exploration, and egalitarian values at the center of college life—no small achievement, especially for a public institution.

If a visionary educator or altruistic philosophy is regarded as a precondition for founding a truly distinctive college, then the College of the Atlantic reminds us that generalizations are always dangerous. These elements would come, but the origins of this college were starkly pragmatic.

Mt. Desert Island sits off the central Maine coast, a granite fortress that is home to the town of Bar Harbor, Acadia National Park, and thousands of summering tourists each year. But the island is something of a human desert in the off season, notwithstanding efforts of the Rockefeller family to establish a clean winter economy to support the local residents.

In 1967 two old schoolmates, Bar Harbor businessman Les Brewer and Father Jim Gower, the new parish priest, pondered once again the dilemma of creating a year-round economy on Mt. Desert Island (Aronow 1983). Why not create a college? The rhythms of academic life would fit perfectly around the season of summer recreation in Bar Harbor. The idea was not new; the chamber of commerce had even discussed the possibility in the past, but now the time was propitious.

Gower and Brewer recruited several other friends, and the group quickly became serious. They constituted themselves legally as a board of trustees, contacted the owners of an abandoned Catholic seminary nearby, and soon had themselves a campus. The old seminary facility was leased for five years "for a dollar a year, plus taxes" (Aronow 1983, p. 8). The founding board included lyricist Eddie Hayman, who suggested the name **"College of the Atlantic"** because the words would lend themselves easily to a school song, if ever one was needed. The future college now had a name, a board of trustees, and a campus. Aside from providing winter employment on Mt. Desert Island, however, it still had no purpose—much less an educational philosophy.

A charter member of the board later reflected that "Father Jim should be given credit for giving the first impetus to the thought of ecology as an area of focus. He had read a new section in *Time* magazine on ecology, which can be defined as a study of our environment" (Aronow 1983, p. 9). The board simply expanded on the idea from the biological sciences to include the human element as well—and "human ecology" became the philosophical center of College of the Atlantic. Oceanography was the other foci, and art and design also were added during the planning stage (p. 9).

It now was time to hire a president to lead the planning process and hire the faculty. By this time, the College of the Atlantic had captured the imagination of many educators and there was no shortage of sitting college presidents among the aspiring candidates. But the board hired   Edward Kaelber   a Harvard professor who had specialized in establishing educational programs in developing countries. "As time went on," Kaelber   remembers, "my definition of human ecology changed. . . ." At the core of the school's mission is what he called "intellectual generosity . . . a real sympathy and an effort to try to understand other ideas; a willingness to give of yourself and to take from others what they want to give" (Aronow 1983, p. 12). Giving generously in proportion to what one receives became the educational creed.

In September 1972, just five years after Les Brewer and Jim Gower first contemplated creating a school, the College of the Atlantic opened its doors. Four faculty who had been chosen to run a pilot summer program in 1971 came back, and 10 more were hired before classes opened in the fall of '72. More than 1,800 aspiring professors had applied.

From the beginning, students were regarded as full partners in building the college—from designing the curriculum to forging fiscal policies. Almost everything was and is done by committee; committee reports are submitted to the All College Meeting, in which every student, faculty member, and administrator participates. Students contribute individually to the welfare of the college as well—each senior is required to carry out a service project that benefits the college, the local community, or the larger global village. The interdisciplinary curriculum at the College of the Atlantic remains focused on marine studies, environmental and biological sciences, public policy, creative arts, environmental design, culture and consciousness, education, and writing (Aronow 1983; McCarthy

1990; Moon 1990).

After two decades of development, the College of the Atlantic graduates about 45 or 50 students each spring. The student body remains at about 250. The college may have started without a visionary leader or educational mission, but a happy convergence of geography and talent led to the identification and articulation of a mission that is exquisitely appropriate to our time. Now fully accredited and well regarded, the College of the Atlantic has earned its place as one of the nation's stable and successful distinctive colleges (College of the Atlantic Catalog 1990-91; McCarthy 1990).

Cases in Context: Life Cycles of Distinctive Colleges

Building a distinctive college, whether it is a new institution or a new initiative within an existing one, requires courage, foresight, and energy. It appears, therefore, that some combination of three factors often is present when distinctive colleges are spawned.

The first factor is a disruption in the larger social fabric—as was present in pre-Civil War America, the opening decades of this century, the Great Depression of the 1930s, the turbulent 1960s, and, probably, our emerging response to global-scale environmental perils. Ferment over fundamental issues of liberty, equality, and justice often produce passionate responses, and higher education often is seen as a primary arena for addressing social discontent.

Fiscal, management, or academic crises within a college constitute a second important factor. When bankruptcy threatens, accreditation is lifted, and a college teeters on the edge of existence, board members and faculty members suddenly may become receptive to educational ideas and methods that would not warrant their glance in good times. Stringfellow Barr and Scott Buchanan were utterly incapable of instituting their neo-classical curriculum at the confident and healthy University of Virginia, but the dispirited professors at St. John's College (at least those who had not already left) took Barr and Buchanan's reform medicine in desperation.

Widespread concern about failures in the higher education system itself is a third important impetus for the development of distinctive colleges. Neglect of liberal education, faculty preoccupation with research, excessive specialization in knowledge and inquiry, and growing impersonalization of instruction continue to cause public and student distress.

These social and academic trends have generally accelerated through the 20th century. Whatever their economic benefits, few educators contest the unfortunate consequences of these changes for undergraduate education.

From the Yale Report in 1828 to the Morrill Federal Land Grant Act of 1862, and from Robert Hutchins to John Dewey in this century, most of those who have done battle over a philosophy for undergraduate education seem to have worked from a common premise—that large classes, passive learning, standardized tests, and professional and vocational training are *not* acceptable practices for the education of college students. Reformers like Meiklejohn, Hutchins, Dewey, Rice, and Barr may have had bitter words for one another, but they also seemed to enjoy an unspoken camaraderie in protesting what they all regarded as the inadequate and even immoral establishment. Together, they were proponents of what Gerald Grant and David Riesman described in their landmark book, *The Perpetual Dream*, as "telic reforms," or reforms based on a philosophy of education (1978).

Changes based simply on pragmatic considerations like student recruitment or those that merely tinker with existing conditions by adding new teaching incentives are another matter. By putting educational values above fiscal considerations or faculty research productivity, telic reforms are inherently risky, even as they promise—and sometimes deliver—major advantages for the students fortunate enough to experience them.

Telic reforms within major universities, such as Meiklejohn's Experimental College at Wisconsin and Hutchins' College at the University of Chicago, sometimes fare better than independent experimental colleges. Brave attempts to create distinctive colleges within large universities—exemplified by interdisciplinary cooperation, teaching innovation, and experiential integration—continue to occur. The Western College Program at Miami University in Ohio and Fairhaven College at Western Washington University in Bellingham are noteworthy examples. They and others like them affect permanent changes in the values and orientations of other faculty, and they serve students well. They also continue to remind everyone—from the board of trustees on down—that the specialized, passive factory model of higher education is inadequate to the development of healthy human beings.

As we reflect on the life cycle of distinctive colleges and

programs, we must recognize an option between the two poles that we have just considered—between maintaining a distinctive character over a period of years and experiencing the death of an experimental institution. The middle ground, not represented by any of the institutions discussed in this section, is occupied by colleges that gradually forfeit their distinctive characteristics. It is quite possible, in other words, to start with a bold plan, but gradually to abandon distinctive practices to economize or to compete in faculty recruitment—until the distinctive characteristics have partially or largely washed out.

Finally, we should look at some of the important differences among distinctive colleges. While many grant students unusual freedom in selecting their course of study and designing their education, others have rejected the elective system and prescribe the curriculum in great detail. Experiential education and service learning may be common, but they are not universal characteristics of distinctive institutions.

Another dimension on which our distinctive colleges displayed philosophical differences is in their attitude toward research. Most of them show hostility—not to research itself, but to research as a mission of their institution or their faculty. Yet a few see research as a means to get students and faculty together in intellectual activity and even in physical work. Reed College and the College of the Atlantic diverge from the norm of most other distinctive colleges in their explicit efforts to integrate research with teaching, especially with advanced students.

The degree to which distinctive colleges follow a progressive or "whole person" approach to education as contrasted with a more intellectual or neo-classical philosophy relates in some degree to the responsiveness of the school to the environment in which it is located. Many distinctive colleges have specifically tailored their educational processes, if not their educational principles, to the land and people of their region. Deep Springs capitalizes on its wilderness location to enable students to experience much of what they study. The same is true of the College of the Atlantic, poised on the wild north Atlantic coast. Berea College has adapted its mission specifically to the Appalachian region—even more to its human ecology than to its natural ecology.

On the other hand, Evergreen State College and the earlier experiments of Meiklejohn and Hutchins were less tailored to their geography. At the far extreme again is St. John's College, which seems not to have adapted its educational program to fit the distinctive environments of its two vastly different campuses in Maryland and New Mexico. The neoclassical approach of St. John's regards education chiefly as a cognitive endeavor that can take place anywhere, irrespective of its setting. For institutions, however, that view education as involving a student's total experience—as at Deep Springs College or the College of the Atlantic—the physical environment is of central importance.

Summary

Some visionaries, like Robert Maynard Hutchins, Stringfellow Barr, and Scott Buchanan, believed human dignity is served best by drawing from the wisdom of the past and projecting the students so educated toward the future. Others, like John Dewey, Joseph Tussman, and the eclectic founders of the College of the Atlantic, believed that immersion in contemporary problems and real experience develop understanding and creativity that best promises to strengthen the individual and the community and address the problems of human dignity and survival.

Almost all distinctive colleges agree that education needs to be more fully engaging of students' intellect and values, more interdisciplinary in the embrace of ideas and application of concepts, and more participatory in the sense that students and faculty are engaged together in teaching and learning. Further, distinctive colleges often converge on the importance of achieving some measure of parity among faculty in salary and rank, muting or eliminating departmental control of the curriculum, preparing students for life primarily and employment secondarily, and subjugating grades and degrees to learning and personal growth.

Distinctiveness often begins as a response to a crisis in the social order—in higher education as a whole or in the life of a particular institution. We must ask, then, whether the urban malaise and ecological crises of the 1990s, coupled with the increased public criticism of colleges and universities, provide new opportunities for birthing distinctive colleges. Our review of the literature and history of telic reforms in undergraduate education suggests a positive response.

THE LURE AND PERILS OF THE QUEST

Many administrators and faculty yearn to lead or be part of a distinctive college or university. What they may not realize is that distinctiveness provides no guarantee of success, as the recounting of the fate of Meiklejohn's Experimental College and Black Mountain College suggests in Section 2. In this section, we set forth some advantages and disadvantages of distinctiveness and explore some factors that facilitate or hamper the quest for distinctiveness.

Some Advantages and Disadvantages of Institutional Distinctiveness

Within the hierarchy of the American higher education system, individual colleges and universities struggle to survive, to preserve their position, or to strengthen it. For colleges and universities concerned about survival, being viewed as distinctive may seem to be the answer. Distinctiveness can indeed attract human and financial resources necessary for survival. For other schools that are more secure financially, the lure of institutional distinctiveness is its connotation of excellence and quality and the consequent improvement of a college or university's status within the educational hierarchy (Carnegie Council 1980).

Possessing a distinctive identity does simplify recruiting students and faculty. The beacon of a specific set of values attracts individuals sympathetic to those values just as it warns off those who are not. Maharishi International University draws individuals who value transcendental meditation, "the experiential component" of the Science of Creative Intelligence taught at the university (Rowe 1980, p. 82). Those who have no interest in transcendental meditation will look elsewhere when selecting a college. Reed College and St. John's, with their image of existing for the intellectually elite, will not attract those who seek big-time sports.

Students and faculty who are drawn to an institution for its distinctive qualities will have made a good match and are likely to stay at the institution and sustain the campus culture and ethos. Membership in colleges such as Berea, Deep Springs, or Alverno may be seen as "part of a special calling" (Templin 1989). The resultant *esprit de corps* aids in times of adversity as well as in day-to-day activities (Rice and Austin 1988; Tierney 1989).

Distinctiveness also aids development activities. Appeals for funds can be targeted to those constituencies that value the school's particular vision of higher education. This targeted approach may yield better results than efforts directed at large.

Finally, distinctiveness may aid decisionmaking, since managerial decisions will be guided by the institution's overarching vision. One response institutional leaders sometimes make to declining finances caused by state budgetary crises, decreased political support, or lowered enrollments is to add programs that they believe will attract students (Cameron 1984; Chaffee 1984). Having a guiding vision for the college or university aids leaders in deciding which programs should be added or deleted.

Conversely, being all things to all people may no longer be possible for many comprehensive colleges and universities. The rapid expansion of size and missions that took place in the 1960s and 1970s is a thing of the past, and downsizing in number of programs—if not in enrollments—may be a key to survival. Determining which programs to keep and which to jettison is easier when institutional leaders evaluate programs in terms of their centrality to the school's educational vision (Kuh, Schuh, Whitt, and Associates 1991). Also, at the state or system level, it becomes easier to allocate resources when they are distributed to complement institutional distinctiveness (Morgan and Newell 1981).

Kalamazoo College is an institution that has accrued several of the benefits of distinctiveness. Almost 30 years ago, Kalamazoo College decided to "bet the whole store on a single vision of education" (Barrett 1990, p. 2). Feeling stretched too thin in its efforts to have comprehensive program offerings, the college community committed itself anew to its tradition of providing a liberal arts curriculum in an environment conducive to the teaching-learning process. As part of the Kalamazoo Plan adopted in the early 1960s, the academic calendar was changed to four 11-week quarters, with students spending one term each year in an off-campus learning experience. During their junior year, all students were required to study abroad.

While these and other changes were not revolutionary, they are manifestations of the college's desire to focus upon what it believes it can and should do well: teach the liberal arts to traditional-age students in a residential setting. Among the benefits of adopting this plan have been not only a solid increase in enrollments but also increasing selectivity in admissions and an increase in financial support (Barrett 1990).

Although institutional distinctiveness can indeed be beneficial, it may be noted that distinctiveness also has its perils not apparent at first glance. One disadvantage is the "competitive paradox" (Anderson 1978, p. 30). According to economic price theory, a product must be distinctive if it is to sell at a price higher than the going market rate. When this theory is applied to the system of higher education, the private sector—traditionally more expensive than the public sector—must be perceived as offering a distinctive education in order for the public to pay the extra cost of attending private schools. However, on the level of the individual private institution, "the more distinctive the college, the smaller the potential market for students and the more difficult it is to maintain enrollments" (p. 30). Single-sex and religious colleges and universities are especially vulnerable to this paradox. The narrowness of their "niche width" is a factor in their generally small size (Meyer and Zucker 1989, p. 71).

Another disadvantage of distinctiveness is a lessened ability to change and adapt to emerging environmental forces (Tierney 1989). Inhibited by an "organizational memory" of what it has been and currently is (Cameron 1984, p. 139), a distinctive college or university may be less equipped to survive in today's rapidly changing, post-industrial environment.

A strong commitment to a vision or the leader that embodies that vision "may prevent shifts to new organizational patterns or practices when new conditions render the old features dysfunctional" (Kaufman 1991, p. 74). Change inconsistent with the school's distinctive character may be resisted internally even when the features that make the institution distinctive are no longer sufficiently valued by many of its constituencies. For survival, a college or university may have to ignore its past values and begin a commitment to new values more appropriate to the current environment.

Related to this lessened ability to be adaptive is the "dilemma of distinction":

The college that strikes boldly for a highly distinctive character and a unique image is also making connections with the outside world that are not easily revoked. The highly distinctive college has a potent claim for attention, but it also

A strong commitment to a vision or the leader that embodies that vision "may prevent shifts to new organizational patterns or practices when new conditions render the old features dysfunctional."

brands itself in the eyes of the world as that kind of place
(Clark 1968, p. 187).

Externally an institution's distinctive image acts as a "constraint" to desired changes in the image (p. 187). For example, if a college becomes known in the general public's mind as having distinctive student-teacher relationships such as students interacting with faculty as equals, this image may be retained long after the college adopts more traditional patterns of interaction between faculty and students. Constituents who desire traditional faculty-student relationships will not value this school because they still retain an image of it as fostering unconventional or even "inappropriate" faculty-student relationships.

The history of the College of William and Mary illustrates how a particular institution both can benefit from and be hurt by its distinctiveness. In the 19th century, the college was well known for educating many Southern leaders. Its "distinctive historical ethos" enabled William and Mary "to accomplish much with few resources" during a key period in its existence. However, the "tradition that identified the school so closely with the Confederate cause also largely explains why the college met such signal failure in its attempt to attract Northern funds after the war" (Smith 1980, pp. 62-3). Northerners were not disposed to aid an institution so closely associated with Southern aristocracy.

A strong institutional tradition can make a college or university distinctive, but distinctiveness based largely on tradition can alienate constituencies that do not value the tradition.

The fate of Parsons College illustrates how a leader's efforts to create a distinctive institution may even contribute to the school's demise. Established in 1875 and affiliated with the Presbyterian Church, Parsons first was accredited in 1913. A Midwestern liberal arts college, it was close to extinction when Millard G. Roberts became its president in 1955. Committed to the principles of corporate management, Roberts cut the number of course offerings, increased the faculty-student ratio, and ensured that the facilities were used day and night. Additionally, Roberts also committed the college to a particular educational vision: working with the "marginal" student (Boroff 1961, p. 105).

Opening the college's door to students not normally admitted to higher education enabled the college to go from fewer than 500 students in 1955 to over 5,000 in the mid-1960s (Boroff 1961). Roberts saw to it that academically weak students were not brought in and then neglected; they were required to spend their first semester in remedial work. Additionally, they jointly studied with faculty several great books during the course of an academic year, took core courses, and were assisted by preceptors (Dixon 1983; Sutton 1959).

In spite of these innovations, Parsons College did not endure. Roberts' vision of an open-admissions four-year college was a radical one during the brief period of time when many higher education institutions could afford to be selective (Rudolph 1977). Also, while Parsons College faculty were glad to have jobs, not all were committed to educating marginal students. Probably few of them liked that Parsons ultimately became "famous [or infamous] for its policy of recruiting students who had flunked out of other colleges" (Van Dyne 1973, p. 4).

Roberts was also a better visionary than a manager (Collins 1969). Although he espoused applying business principles to higher education—including the idea that Parsons College could make a profit (Koerner 1969)—ultimately the college foundered because of poor financial management exacerbated by its loss of accreditation. With a history of accreditation problems initiated before Roberts became president, in 1967 Parsons lost its accreditation for failure to "provide an adequate educational program for its students, especially those of limited ability" (Kaplan 1979, p. 443).

Some authors suggest that Parsons lost its accreditation because leaders of other institutions were jealous of the college's success (Collins 1969; Koerner 1969). Whatever the reasons, Parsons's board of trustees fired Roberts in 1967. Regaining its accreditation in 1970, only to lose it again in 1973, Parsons closed that year because of bankruptcy. The campus was sold and is now the site of the Maharishi International University. The demise of Parsons College is testimony to the need to combine an educational vision with sound management practices.

Factors Facilitating and Hampering a Quest For Distinctiveness

What is and what is not distinctive about a college or university is subject to external forces and constituents' expectations of institutions. Certain forces or factors such as whether it is

state owned or independent are inherent to the institution. Other factors affect all schools: failure of relevant constituencies to support innovation, the constraints of regional and programmatic accreditation, and the norms of professional behavior to which the faculty have been socialized.

Whether a college or university is public or private may affect its ability to be distinctive. In general, it seems easier for private colleges and universities to attain distinctiveness (Grant and Riesman 1978). First of all, public institutions are more apt than private ones to be multiple-purpose institutions serving a variety of constituencies. As such, public colleges and universities must respond to numerous interest groups and assume a comprehensive mission (Clark 1968). The resulting diffusion of purpose hampers attempts to achieve distinctiveness through focusing on the needs of a particular constituency such as the extremely academically talented or individuals of a particular ethnic group or gender.

Being required to spread institutional resources so widely can prohibit the concentration of time, effort, and money needed to develop a distinctive approach to student services (Moseley 1988). Furthermore, public colleges and universities are more likely than private ones to be commuter institutions. Non-residential schools are less apt to develop a shared campus culture. Finally, public institutions are usually controlled by state boards or government councils which frequently function to standardize processes and programs at these institutions and may limit their ability to be entrepreneurial (Riesman 1980; Skolnik 1989).

Efforts at institutional distinctiveness also fail if relevant constituencies do not value the elements that make the college or university distinctive, as exemplified by the history of Monteith College. Wayne State University created Monteith College in 1959 to counter the increasing academic specialization and neglect of undergraduates decried in universities (Riesman, Gusfield, and Gamson 1970). Convinced of the value of general education for all students including the non-elite, Monteith was one of the first American institutions to offer a degree in general education. Its curriculum was highly structured, but students also were encouraged to study independently of the formal course structure. To encourage an interdisciplinary approach in courses, the college was organized by divisions rather than departments. The college also was designed to enroll no more than 1,200 students in order to ensure adequate academic and personal attention to students.

Monteith's location within a university contributed to its ability to be distinctive. Students desirous of career preparation had the option of taking courses from other colleges within the university or of transferring to another college if Monteith was not the right fit.

In spite of this advantage, Monteith did not endure. While Riesman, Gusfield, and Gamson (1970) labelled Monteith as "an experiment stabilized" (p. 205), in December 1975 Wayne State's board of trustees voted to eliminate Monteith. At a time when state monies were extremely limited, Monteith's pedagogy was deemed too expensive. Its students, who never numbered more than 800, attended large lectures also attended by 12 to 15 faculty members, who then would meet with the students to discuss the lecture. A faculty-student ratio of 1 to 12-15 students was not deemed viable for a state institution in a financially troubled state. Monteith also was plagued by jealousies within the university, so that university support for its continuance was lacking (Herman 1992; Perus 1978). Monteith's fate sounds a cautionary note to those who seek distinctiveness for their institution.

Like Monteith, Oakland University was distinctive from its inception. Unlike Monteith, Oakland has survived, but in altered form. Established in the late 1950s as an offshoot of Michigan State University, Oakland was created to provide an academically demanding liberal arts education to working class and lower-middle class commuter students of average academic ability. Created in the Sputnik era, the curriculum reflected the national desire for rigorously trained college students. The heart of the curriculum was a general education core which extended over four years and equaled approximately half the credits needed for graduation. The institution itself was to be a small, public liberal arts college that eschewed the traditional collegiate frills of intercollegiate sports and Greek societies.

While the curriculum and faculty standards were appropriate for the kind of institution envisioned, they were not appropriate for the kind of students who enrolled at Oakland. These students were first-generation college students who lived nearby and were attending college to improve their socio-economic position. Oakland was their college choice because of its location, not because of its curriculum. Average in academic ability, they were frustrated by the demanding curriculum and faculty.

As attrition soared and enrollment dropped, changes were made to adapt the curriculum and grading standards to the needs and abilities of Oakland's students (Levine 1978; Riesman, Gusfield, and Gamson 1970). Rather than a set of core courses required of all students, the general education component of the curriculum currently utilizes the distribution model. Additionally, the university offers numerous programs designed to meet the students' interest in career education. Independent from Michigan State as of 1970, Oakland had a 1991-92 enrollment of 12,400 students; 69 percent had an ACT score at or over 21 (Dilts 1991).

Oakland had to let go of its distinctive curriculum in order to have a thriving enrollment and a satisfactory retention rate. In following the distribution model, Oakland's general education curriculum now is like that of the majority of four-year colleges (Levine 1978). The homogeneity of most institutions' general education component of the curriculum is but one illustration of the increasing homogeneity of American colleges and universities on certain dimensions such as academic programs and student services. While some of this homogeneity is attributable to the growth in state and federal control of higher education (Millet 1985; Rossman and El-Khawas 1987), regional and programmatic accrediting associations also may have contributed to this homogenization. Institutional and programmatic adherence to the standards and criteria for accreditation can lead to standardization of both the "input" and "output" as well as the educational process itself (Koerner 1971; Zoffer 1987).

John F. Kennedy University is a non-traditional university that is becoming more traditional because of the demands of a regional accrediting body, the Western Association of Schools and Colleges (WASC). Established in 1965 to educate adults, the university is atypical in several respects. Without a campus, the university accommodates its student body, which is largely female (70 percent) and older (average age is 37) in classes offered in evenings and on weekends. The majority of its students (70 percent) are enrolled in graduate programs; the most unusual is a program called the "Study of Human Consciousness." Until 1991, the university was staffed totally by part-time faculty. Because WASC criticized the institution's governance structure on the grounds that faculty were insuffiently involved in curricular decisions, JFK finally has hired 16 full-time faculty and changed some of its governance procedures. Although these changes indeed may be beneficial to the institution and its students, they serve to make John F. Kennedy University more traditional in its approach to higher education (DeLoughry 1992).

Standardized definitions of excellence also may inhibit development of institutional distinctiveness—at least in certain institutional types. By adopting knowledge production as its primary value, the professoriate in research and doctoral-granting universities and in elite liberal arts colleges has standardized its criteria for excellence within the profession. These faculty attend to the norms of their academic discipline and usually value achievement within that discipline as opposed to institutional norms and achievement. Faculty's disciplinary rather than institutional focus and the professionalization of the faculty have led to the adoption of measures of excellence that are almost the same for these institutional types, regardless of mission or purpose, clientele, or type of control. Efforts to develop a distinctive academic approach in such institutions would be extremely difficult if the approach disregarded traditional criteria of excellence (Adams 1984; Grant and Riesman 1978; Jencks and Riesman 1968; Martin 1969; Skolnik 1989).

The University of California at Santa Cruz is a university that was created in the 1960s to embody the values of the counterculture that since has become increasingly traditional in its orientation due to "the professional interests of the academic culture" (Adams 1984). Dedicated to undergraduate liberal education as opposed to the multiversity's emphasis on research and the professions, Santa Cruz sought to develop a sense of community for its students and faculty. Several colleges, each with its own distinctive curriculum and ethos, were created "not only to foster a sense of belonging and community, but to develop particular styles of intellectual life uniquely suited to the needs of undergraduate teaching and learning" (Adams 1984, p. 23). A narrative evaluation system and intramural and club sports program instead of the standard university sports system enhanced the sense of community rather than competition.

When Santa Cruz first opened, it attracted some of the brightest faculty and students. By the mid-1970s, as high school graduates became more conservative, enrollment dropped. Santa Cruz had developed the image of being "'flaky' and 'touchy feely'" (Adams 1984, p. 20), partly because of its emphasis on "relevant" curriculum and its concern for "intensely personal, immediate, and emotional" knowledge (p. 24). Faculty suffered from their dual commitment to a particular college and to a board of study designed as a kind of departmental structure.

To change its image and to alleviate faculty frustrations and tensions, Santa Cruz shifted to more traditional administrative and curricular patterns: administration became more centralized, the power for curricular decisions shifted from the colleges to the boards of study, and letter grades became a option. "Standards" and "excellence" became part of the institutional rhetoric. Faculty seeking tenure were expected to meet traditional university expectations regarding publication in a specific field. Curricular service to a specific college was devalued and interdisciplinary work was less encouraged. While still an innovative university, Santa Cruz has moved into the mainstream of American higher education as adherence to traditional professional and academic standards has emerged at the institution (Adams 1984; Alpert 1986; Grant and Riesman 1978).

Perceptions of constituencies at Amherst College about Hampshire College (also located in Amherst, Massachusetts) further illustrate the tension between traditional standards and values and non-traditional approaches to higher education. Amherst College has a long tradition as an elite private liberal arts college with traditional standards of excellence suitable for a student body that assumes the bachelor's degree is a step to a graduate or professional degree. Although Hampshire also is an elite private liberal arts college whose students usually go on to graduate or professional school, it arose as a response to student discontent in the 1960s. Opened in 1970, Hampshire envisions the appropriate liberal arts education as one best "shaped by the student's own interests" (Hampshire College 1992 Undergraduate Catalogue).

Working within an interdisciplinary framework, students determine an area of concentration and contract with a faculty committee appropriate learning activities for this interest. The culminating experience in their concentration is a major independent study project. The college culture emphasizes the teaching-learning process, close faculty-student relationships, self-motivation, creativity, and independent study (Gamson and Associates 1984). A sense of community is emphasized by requiring students to participate in community service and study Third World and minority cultures (Hampshire College 1992 Undergraduate Catalogue).

From Amherst's perspective, "Hampshire's curriculum is trendy, its standards lax, its faculty composed largely of ideologues and misfits; [and] its students take their education casually and are given credit for almost everything" (Meister 1982, p. 27). From Hampshire's perspective, Amherst is "a bastion of cultural elitism and authoritarian pedagogy; its curriculum avoids engagement with social issues; [and] its standards are rigid." Additionally, "its faculty is composed largely of ivory tower, Platonic academics; its students are . . . given credit for nothing except what transpires in the classroom" (pp. 27-8).

A shared vision and purpose unifies college or university constituents.

Amherst College represents the university model of higher education, while Hampshire represents an alternative paradigm, what Grant and Riesman (1978) label as "communal-expressive" in their discussion of "telic reforms." As indicated in Section 2, few colleges and universities implement or embody telic reform; most accept the goals of research universities and at best modify themselves through "popular reforms" such as student-designed majors and minimal curricular requirements (Grant and Riesman 1978, p. 16). Using this framework, we can see that highly distinctive colleges and universities probably will run counter to the mainstream of American higher education. Being outside the mainstream has both advantages and disadvantages, as we have noted.

Summary

A shared vision and purpose unifies college or university constituents. They also contribute to institutional survival or increased status. These benefits lie behind the frequent urging of higher education leaders to strive for institutional distinctiveness.

Those interested in achieving distinctiveness need to assess the likelihood that their college or university will become distinctive. Certain factors such as mode of institutional control and normative and structural openness to change affect this. These factors are difficult to manipulate or control.

Even if it were possible for all colleges and universities to achieve a high degree of distinctiveness, some institutional leaders might not hold this as a goal. There is a down side

to being distinctive. A high degree of distinctiveness can limit a school's appeal to various constituencies as well as its ability to adapt to emerging environmental forces.

STRATEGIC MANAGEMENT AND INSTITUTIONAL DISTINCTIVENESS

If convinced that their college or university both could and should be distinctive, leaders may ask, "What strategies might we follow to actually make this school more distinctive?" Drawing from the theoretical traditions of strategic management, we will construct a framework that makes it possible to define what distinguishes the distinctive college or university from one that simply is different. Specifically, we will examine two major strategic management paradigms for their relationship to institutional distinctiveness and suggest that, for most colleges and universities, distinctiveness requires a merging of the two paradigms.

Paradigms for Strategic Management

Whether addressed to business or higher education leaders, the strategic management literature reflects two opposing organizational and management models: the adaptive and the interpretive (Chaffee 1984; Keeley 1988). The adaptive model considers the organization as a whole; the interpretive is concerned most with the individuals in the organization. Understanding these two paradigms is fundamental to understanding institutional distinctiveness. The two models can be used together to produce a strategy for distinctiveness.

The adaptive model regards organizations as living organisms with rationally defined goals achievable through the collective efforts of team members. Leaders are expected to assess trends in the environment and adapt the organization to new needs to meet its desired outcome (e.g., Keller 1983; Kotler and Murphy 1981). For businesses, that outcome usually is profit. For colleges and universities, the outcome is student enrollments, contributions to the endowment, and a balanced budget.

All organizations must acquire enough resources to function. Organizational leaders, therefore, must strive to keep an institution in tune with its environment and its market. The key organizational question for those managing by the adaptive model is, "What are we doing?" (Chaffee 1984, p. 221). The adaptive model emphasizes the organization as a whole unit.

The interpretive model emphasizes individuals. Organizations are seen as networks of individuals who choose to work together because doing so satisfies personal needs.

[T]he purpose as well as the binding element of social organization is the satisfaction of diverse individual interests" (Keeley 1988, p. 32).

The leader's role is to interpret the needs and desires of people who have a stake in the organization, both internally and externally. Leaders must weave individual needs into a fabric or culture strong enough to sustain the organization (Pfeffer 1981; Smirich and Morgan 1982). The organization is held together by a social contract among its members.

The interpretive model depends on finding and expressing common values and creating a culture that justifies individual commitments. Leaders define the values that unify efforts and tell the "story" that gives each member a sense of direction and ownership. The question that guides action is, "Why are we together?" (Chaffee 1984, p. 221).

The adaptive and interpretive strategies are not mutually exclusive. In her study of the strategic management of 14 small, private colleges that had undergone decline, Chaffee categorized their management strategies as either adaptive or interpretive to determine which type of management worked better to turn the college around (1984). She found that all of the colleges used adaptive strategies—but some also used interpretive strategies. Those that used both together recovered more quickly from decline. Chaffee concluded that "turnaround management in private colleges is most effective when participants think of the organization simultaneously as an organism and as a social contract" (p. 228).

Most of the strategies proposed for higher education during the last decade have been rooted in the adaptive theory and have emulated business organizations and their tactics (e.g., Hossler and Bean 1990; Keller 1983; Kotler and Fox 1985). We will briefly explore adaptive strategy in the world of business and discuss how this line of thinking has been fitted to higher education.

Adaptive Strategy in Business
To be successful, businesses must offer a product or service perceived by consumers as providing the best "value" for the money. Some consumers may value low cost over high quality, while others value style or uniqueness over low cost. A successful product or service provides the desired level of value to a particular group of consumers. The trick is to read

the needs and aspirations of a potential market, given social trends and business competition. In his consideration of competitive strategy, Michael Porter suggests that businesses can achieve a superior long-term return on investment by one of two ways (1980).

According to the Porter Generic Model illustrated in figure 1, one business may aim for a high market share in the industry if enough individuals desiring the product place importance on availability and affordability. For example, Emerson Electric has been able to gain a large portion of the market for electronic products by recognizing that many consumers want an affordable product that fulfills the basic need. Emerson, therefore, gains competitive advantage by offering an acceptable level of quality at a very low price (cost leadership strategy).

FIGURE 1

THE PORTER GENERIC STRATEGY MODEL

Competitive Scope	Competitive Advantage	
	Low cost	**Differentiation**
Broad Target	Cost leadership Strategy	**Differentiation Strategy**
Narrow Target	Cost Focus Strategy	**Differentiation Focus Strategy**

Source: Michael E. Porter, *Competitive Advantage: Creating and Sustaining Superior Performance* (New York: Free Press, 1985, p. 12). Reprinted with permission of the Free Press, division of MacMillan, Inc.

Another business may aim for a high market share by providing a special quality or feature that has market appeal. Consumers usually are willing to pay a little more to get a product that uniquely fits their need. Caterpillar Tractor has established a "differentiated advantage" in the marketplace by recognizing customers' need for a dealer system that brings high quality equipment and spare parts close to the place of equipment use (differentiation strategy).

Alternatively, long-term financial gains can be achieved through a "focus" strategy. Using this strategy, a firm will con-

centrate on the unique needs of a specific market niche. The goal is not to win high market share. Rather, the hope is to develop a product so completely geared to the need of a select group of people that the firm will win their business. If that niche demands a low price strategy, the firm will try to provide the demanded level of quality at the lowest possible price. La Quinta Motor Inns has selected to serve a very specific group (traveling salespeople) and to meet this group's basic needs (and nothing more) at a low price (cost focus strategy).

However, when a specific target group demands a certain deviation from the norm and is willing to pay a premium price for that value, a differentiated focus strategy is executed. Cray Computer has established a competitive advantage by concentrating on delivering one product to a narrowly defined niche of need. Cray's business is to produce the best "super computers" in the world. High market share in the general computer business is not the aim. The goal is to produce superior results by focusing attention on the very specific needs of a small portion of the broad market (differentiation focus strategy).

The Porter Generic Model is a framework consistent with the adaptive paradigm. The model suggests that a well-executed strategy to establish a competitive advantage will increase a business's chances for financial stability. The firms most in danger financially are those that lack a clear differentiated advantage, low cost advantage, or a focus strategy. In times of intense competition, they are "stuck in the middle" (Porter 1980, p. 41) trying to be all things to all markets, copying the strategy of the industry's leaders, or lacking any true advantage.

Adaptive Strategy in Higher Education

Applied to higher education, the Porter Generic Model illustrated in figure 2 suggests that a college or university can develop a strategy to establish some basis for institutional advantage in the marketplace.

The need for affordable, accessible education provides an opportunity for a cost leadership strategy shown in position 1 in figure 2. Some colleges and universities may make education more physically accessible to students, thus decreasing the time and money associated with obtaining a college education. If the school can provide the desired level of quality

FIGURE 2
PORTER GENERIC MODEL APPLIED TO HIGHER EDUCATION STRATEGY

Competitive Scope	Competitive Advantage	
	Low cost	Differentiation*
National/Regional	Cost leadership Strategy	Differentiation Strategy
	Position 1	Position 2
Particular Segment of Group	Cost Focus Strategy	Differentiation Focus Strategy
	Position 2	Position 4

* Differentiation perceived by constituency

at a lower per-student cost, it has the basis to suggest to the market that it is able to provide a better "value" to the student.

Mercy College provides an example of a college that used aggressive planning to make higher education accessible to students by taking the institution to the students. Using extension centers and offering courses at six correctional facilities, Mercy was able to grow from 1,500 students in 1972 to more than 9,500 students a decade later (Kemerer, Baldridge, and Green 1982).

Similarly, Georgia State University has set out to be that state's "low tuition cost and high quality instruction [institution with] flexible scheduling [and] easy access" (Hossler and Bean 1990, p. 120). Located in the state's capital, the university has been able to sell itself to a regional, national, and even international market.

Leaders may recognize an opportunity to differentiate and gain regional or even national acclaim by developing a unique offering or superior quality (see position 3 in figure 2). The plan may be to claim an advantage that is institutional in nature.

For example, doctoral-granting universities may launch strategies to become established research institutions to win some of the credibility and esteem enjoyed by research universities. Other schools respond to the cry for improved teaching by developing a regional reputation for teaching excellence. The key strategic element is to discover a broad marketplace need that a school can use to garner a regional or national constituency.

The conditions at many colleges and universities are not conducive to the development of a national institutional reputation. These schools may implement an incremental differentiation strategy by developing selected programs for different audiences (Morgan and Newell 1981). Developing programmatic advantage may be easier for more comprehensive institutions than developing a single, unifying theme (Gamson and Associates 1984).

Thus, a community college may develop a support program for women and men returning to school after at least a five-year absence, as San Jose Community College has done (Dzierlendga 1981); a comprehensive college receptive to the needs of non-traditional students could develop degree programs aimed solely at part-time students who are working adults, as Elmhurst College has done (Elmhurst College Catalog 1989). In recent years, some colleges and universities have even used athletics as a means to establish a differentiated advantage.

Another strategy is to reject comprehensiveness and focus energies and resources upon a kind of education (Mayhew 1974; Moseley 1988). The differentiation focus strategy (position 4 in figure 2) first calls for selecting a definite target audience to serve and then delivering a type of education that fits the needs of that particular constituency. Military academies provide a uniquely designed educational experience for those aspiring to a career in the armed forces. Church-related institutions also usually pursue a focus strategy.

Colleges and universities pursuing this strategy choose not to compete in the broad market. Instead, they isolate a niche of need they are able to satisfy and concentrate on that need. By identifying a group to serve, understanding the aspirations of that particular group, and then developing an educational product that fits this group's needs, a college or university is more likely to create a culture within the constituency that produces long-term institutional support. Also, the advice to focus on a specific educational purpose is consistent with the planning literature that urges the development of a clear mission (e.g., Cable 1984; Keller 1983; Richman and Farmer 1976).

As was true for institutions striving to obtain broad market appeal, the focus strategy may result in a low cost advantage or a differentiated advantage. The demand of the particular market may require a low cost strategy (position 2 in figure 2).

Olivet Nazarene University promotes itself as having the lowest tuition cost among Illinois private colleges and universities. Olivet is targeted, however, to the specific educational aspirations of the members of the owning church. Its strategy is contrasted with the differentiated strategy of Wheaton College, which focuses on attracting high-ability students who want to study in a purposely designed evangelical environment (position 4).

The focus strategy does introduce an element of additional risk, however. Colleges and universities pursuing a focus strategy become dependent on the fortunes of the particular niche. Any changes in the group or its perceived needs can doom the institution.

Many schools in recent years have relinquished their focus strategy in light of changing demographics and constituency aspirations and have become comprehensive colleges or universities. According to the logic of Porter's model, this move only increases the probability that the college or university will lack a long-term competitive advantage. Other schools have redirected their strategy to a new segment of unmet need. For example, recent years have seen a trend for denominational colleges once dedicated to a particular religious group to re-target efforts to another niche of need—the adult learner and degree-completion programs.

The model for competitive advantage calls on colleges and universities to analyze the market opportunities and then cut a trail away from the norms of the day by identifying a specific focus for attention. The thinking that leads to a focus strategy also is consistent with the adaptive paradigm of strategy. It is grounded in a belief that an organization is an entity with the goal of acquiring the required level of resources. It does so by reacting to environmental changes and anticipating needs and by adjusting strategy so that the organization will continue to prosper. Use of the adaptive paradigm guided by the logic of the Porter Generic Model is likely to increase the probability of a school's success and to contribute to the diversity of higher education as a system. Yet this path does not produce institutional distinctiveness.

The Interpretive Model and Institutional Distinctiveness

We believe the interpretive paradigm holds out the best promise of achieving distinctiveness. The distinctive institution is a product of a social contract among colleagues to organize their efforts around a unifying purpose. In so doing, all members are involved in a task which they believe to be in their self-interest. As long as they believe this, there is commitment to the course of action. Strategy is the statement of a "reason for being," the clarification of its meaning, and the organization of tasks to accomplish the vision.

The relationship between unifying purpose and the development of a college's distinctiveness was first set forth in Clark's *The Distinctive College* (1970), a study of the distinctive private liberal arts college as exemplified by Reed, Antioch, and Swarthmore. Here, Clark posits the thesis that "the central ingredient in the making of the distinctive college" (p. 8) is the organizational saga, the legend that has developed about the institution and which reflects the institution's values. A "unifying and motivating theme" (p. 236) is critical to the development of a distinctive college, for it is this theme that becomes the basis of the legend or saga.

Development of an organizational saga may occur under one of three institutional conditions: (1) the creation of a new organization; (2) a crisis in an established organization; or (3) evolution within an established organization. In each instance there must be "a normative as well as a structural openness" (p. 240) that permits an individual to introduce and implement his or her unifying theme for several years. Whether motivated by concerns about institutional survival or stagnation or by an inspiring vision for a new institution, college constituencies must be open to change. Likewise, the organizational structure must not be so rigid that change is impossible or highly unlikely.

Development and entrenchment of unifying themes occur in stages. First, a leader offers a vision for the college or university. This leader is not necessarily the president. As philanthropists providing the money to found the institutions named after them, Leland Stanford and Ezra Cornell were influential in the initial guiding visions for these schools (Brubacher and Rudy 1976). Even if not the source of the vision, the president must articulate and endorse the unifying vision or theme.

Next, a core of senior faculty must adopt, espouse, and focus their energies on advancing the vision. Their reluctance to do so can delay or deter implementation of the president's vision. Given this faculty commitment, the curriculum, programs, and services must reflect the values inherent in the institutional vision.

Those outside the institution, particularly its alumni, must become committed to the theme. This development of a supportive external social base enables the institution to "achieve a differentiated, protected position in the markets and organizational complexes that allocate money, personnel, and students" (p. 250). Within the institution, a student subculture that assimilates the theme's values must develop. Finally, "the saga itself—as ideology, self-image, and public image" (p. 246) must gain a "forceful momentum" (p. 246), affecting both the college members and the external social base. Only a vision whose "ideals . . . fit the institutional environment" and which is "appropriate to the students being taught" will ultimately endure (Gamson and Associates 1984, p. 84).

Thus the starting point for the distinctive institution must be a unifying vision representing institutional members' values. The origin of this vision, however, may come from any number of sources. A distinctive institution may emerge from a specific educational philosophy or tradition. St. John's philosophy that it can best provide for a higher education through a curriculum committed to the "Great Books" or Swarthmore's honors program are two examples of distinctive institutional values connected to a philosophy of education.

The call for distinctiveness is a call for innovation, entrepreneurship, and even educational revolution.

A distinctive institution may arise from a specific social cause or societal need. It may be a function of a devotion to the needs of a particular group. Witness Gallaudet's focus on providing a liberal arts education to the hearing impaired and Landmark's focus on enabling dyslexic students to succeed in traditional academic ways.

Distinctiveness may come from a new educational idea as with Alverno's competency-based education or from loyalty to a traditional ideology applied to non-traditional students as at Brooklyn College. The potential sources for the values shaping distinctiveness are endless. The call for distinctiveness is a call for innovation, entrepreneurship, and even educational revolution.

It is not sufficient for leaders to say college or university constituents are committed to a set of values. The values must guide and direct the actual curriculum, the selection process for faculty and students, the policy and procedures, and the culture. For example, the State University of New York at Stony Brook holds as a value a sense of academic community. A manifestation of this value is its program of Federated Learning Communities designed to create and cultivate a sense of academic community.

Within the program, existing courses are grouped or "federated" according to broad themes such as world hunger. Students who desire to be part of a particular federation enroll in all the courses for a particular theme. The faculty in each federation meet regularly for two years to discuss the courses and the teaching-learning process. An integrative seminar taught by a "master teacher" and graduate student, a core course team-taught by all faculty in the federation, and the opportunity for students to pursue an interdisciplinary project after the federated courses are completed are other aspects of this approach.

Faculty and students alike have been energized by participating in Stony Brook's learning communities, a novel way to avoid the sense of academic isolation often experienced in research universities and to develop and enhance a sense of academic community (Gamson and Associates 1984, pp. 85-86).

Two recent studies also underscore the cultural dynamics that result in distinctiveness. In their study of noteworthy liberal arts colleges, Rice and Austin cite 10 schools such as Smith College, William Jewell, and Greenville that have foregone pragmatic concerns about market share and "competitive edge" and have remained true to a clearly articulated mission carried forward by a distinctive culture (1988, p. 52).

The four institutional features cited as sources of high faculty morale and satisfaction are evidence of the interpretive paradigm: a carefully nurtured organizational culture, participatory leadership, a sense of organizational momentum, and a faculty that identifies with the institution (pp. 2, 8, 9).

The same themes are found in Kuh, Schuh, Whitt, and Associates' (1991) investigation of "involving colleges," institutions that have "a special quality . . ., an intangible something in the woodwork, that sustains the community." This "something special is rooted in the institutional culture and dominant subcultures that promote involvement and a sense of ownership among members" (p. 53). Like Rice and Austin (1988), they note the influence of traditions, rituals, language, architecture, and symbols. Although these institutions' leaders have exemplified the interpretive strategy, they also have developed a competitive advantage for their schools.

In sum, the development of a distinctive institution must be started and grounded in the articulation of educational values that call upon internal constituents to commit to the achievement of these values. The basis for action is the shared commitment of individuals dedicated to a common pursuit.

Distinctiveness: Merging of the Interpretive And Adaptive Views

Distinctive colleges often have been formed by visionaries whose thinking seems consistent with the interpretive paradigm. The story of Black Mountain College illustrates how one individual's values and vision could inspire others to risk the sacrifices necessary to found a new institution. Together, this group of committed individuals created a short-lived distinctive college. The light dimmed and the college failed, however, when its participants no longer were willing to commit to the unifying values.

Another example of an institution whose mission emerged over time through the commitment of individuals is the College of the Atlantic. The presence of Bar Harbor inspired a vision of education in the biological sciences. Individuals' commitment to the concept of "human ecology" gave birth to a unifying value that has produced a distinctive, economically viable college.

The College of the Atlantic also demonstrates how a group of educators, committed to a common vision, can implement a plan that produces distinctiveness and positions the college in an educational niche that enhances its chance of survival. Visionary leadership and market success need not be viewed as mutually exclusive. New management techniques can enable today's visionaries to use sound organizational practices that will ensure the survival and maintenance of their distinctive educational vision.

We suggest that leaders who recognize the potential for distinctiveness within their school or those who hope to more effectively market the reality of a distinctive culture turn to the Porter Generic framework to identify a positioning strategy for their college or university. An example of a distinctive college that has developed an overall cost leadership position is Brooklyn College. Distinctive schools striving for broad appeal with a differentiation strategy are Swarthmore, Alverno College, Bunker Hill Community College, and, possibly, Kalamazoo College.

Historically, most distinctive institutions have reflected focus strategies, usually by providing some unique offering which sometimes justifies a premium price. Several previously mentioned examples are evident: Gallaudet and Landmark. It is possible, however, to focus on the particular needs or aspirations of a small segment with a low-cost position such as Berea College. Thus, it is possible for a college or university to implement a strategy grounded in the interpretative paradigm, centered on core educational values, and implemented in such a way that the school enjoys the necessary level of market acceptance and results in a competitive advantage.

One such institution that has effectively developed a strategy to become the exemplar institution of its type is Miami-Dade Community College. As a multi-purpose two-year college with a non-selective, commuter student body, Miami-Dade Community College would seem to be poorly positioned for acclaim. Yet it has achieved a reputation for educational excellence among community colleges (Rouche and Baker 1987; Zwerling 1988).

Beginning in 1978, students who did not meet certain academic standards after two semesters were dropped from the institution. Although several thousand students were dropped in the first couple of years, Miami-Dade's tightening of standards and raising of academic expectations has resulted in increased respect for the institution among students, prospective students, its community, and the nation at large.

Another part of its commitment to excellence is the college's emphasis on effective teaching. An elaborate system of self-evaluation and documentation of teaching effectiveness is used to identify top faculty, who receive additional salary and status in the form of "teaching chairs" (Kirp 1992). These strategies have helped Miami-Dade grow from an initial enrollment of 1,400 students in 1960 to over 100,000 students annually, making Miami-Dade not only the largest community college but also the largest college in the nation.

Is Miami-Dade a distinctive college? In order to meet the criteria, the values permeating from the organizational culture must manifest themselves in a unifying purpose that forges a social contract among colleagues to organize their efforts around the fulfillment of a particular educational vision. Evidence of this is found in the literature about Miami-Dade. Zwerling (1988) took a skeptical look at Miami-Dade in his qualitative analysis of the culture of the institution and found that faculty commitment to the reforms has resulted in literally hundreds of special programs and initiatives for unique needs and student clienteles.

The "master plan" for reform brought to the institution by President McCabe was refined to match the values of members as he immersed himself in the expectations of the faculty and staff. Over time a plan emerged that reflected the common commitment of internal constituencies. Flowing from this commitment came new energy for strategic and tactical action. Miami-Dade, through its actions, has become a differentiated community college serving the broad market and achieving a national reputation. Miami-Dade is not only distinctive, it also possesses a clear competitive advantage.

• Leaders should consider the tools of adaptive strategic planning when shaping the execution of a strategy for economically viable distinctiveness. The distinctive school will not permit changing market realities and the latest expressed needs to dictate the strategy for that day. Its leaders must match the institution's educational vision to market needs or market the institution to create its own demand.

Summary
We have used the two dominant management strategies, the adaptive and interpretive models, to distinguish between diversity and distinctiveness. When institutional management strategies are viewed from the Porter Generic Strategy Model, it becomes apparent that colleges and universities can follow those that will lead to some form of competitive advantage. Such strategies emerge from the adaptive model; when employed, they add to system diversity and may increase the probability of institutional survival during times of intense competition for constituency support. Such strategies, however, do not produce institutional distinctiveness.

Distinctiveness is a product of thinking consistent with the interpretive strategy of organizational management. The resulting strategic management is centered on a unifying set of values perceived by relevant constituencies as extraordinary in a positive way. Leaders who aspire to distinctiveness for their college or university must clearly state the unifying value(s) around which individuals and institutions will rally and then develop a unique educational offering that fulfills the defined vision.

Ideally, the educational vision that makes a college or university distinctive will be accepted by a portion of the market large enough to ensure that the school can survive. To increase the possibility of success, institutional leaders may be wise to position the strategy in light of the alternative strategies suggested by the Porter Generic model. Truly "distinctive" colleges and universities that survive over the long run are likely to be the result of a merging of the interpretive and the adaptive strategic management paradigms.

CONCLUSIONS AND RECOMMENDATIONS

Can state legislators, system leaders, or individuals committed to a particular educational vision create a distinctive college or university that will succeed in the marketplace? Are there steps that can turn a school that is merely different into one that is distinctive? To answer these questions, we pulled from the higher education literature on distinctiveness and from the strategic management literature to clarify the term "distinctive" in the context of management decisions for colleges and universities.

First, we defined a distinctive college or university as one whose institutional activities reflect and embody a unifying set of values esteemed by both internal and external constituents. Then we distinguished between "distinctive" and "differentiated" institutions to show that many current management decisions are the product of a plan to differentiate. Using differentiation strategy results in a college or university having a competitive edge over others in its group and classification.

However, true distinctiveness does not start in a plan to differentiate. It starts with a commitment to a form of education or an educational belief so compelling that individuals unite to make the vision a reality.

The concepts of distinctiveness and differentiation may not, however, be mutually exclusive. The same steps of market strategy used in a differentiation strategy also could be used by those committed to distinctiveness. We believe that some colleges and universities have the potential to be distinctive, some are distinctive but are not well-marketed, and others are unique but not distinctive. To help leaders uncover whether a college or university has the potential for distinctiveness and how feasible this distinctiveness is in the marketplace, we have developed an action plan that draws from the adaptive and interpretive models of strategic management.

A Plan for Deciding Whether to Pursue Distinctiveness

Underlying our plan to uncover or make explicit a college or university's distinctiveness are two assumptions. First, presidents lead by articulating themes and focusing attention on values already inherent in the institution (Birnbaum 1992). Leaders who try to plant an educational vision inconsistent with a college or university's values may find rocky, unreceptive soil. External constituents may perceive an illusion of distinctiveness—to the current leader's glory, but it will not survive past the leader's term in office.

Next, "ceaselessly vigilant leadership" (Grant and Riesman 1978, p. 309) is necessary for colleges and universities to maintain their distinctiveness. Remember that schools that begin as nationally distinctive may not endure as illustrated by the histories of Black Mountain College, Monteith College, and Meiklejohn's Experimental College at the University of Wisconsin, and Hutchins' undergraduate College at the University of Chicago. If such institutions endure, they may have to modify their distinctive nature to stabilize their finances and maintain enrollments, as witness the histories of Oakland and Santa Cruz. In short, genuine and enduring distinctiveness is slowly constructed, carefully nurtured, and cannot be forced.

Systemic and institutional leaders interested in nurturing a distinctive institution should consider doing the following:

1. *Conduct historical and cultural analyses to uncover the college or university's institutional values.* The distinctiveness strategy starts with the deliberate discovery of shared institutional values that can result in a unifying vision of education.

   Because a basis for distinctiveness likely will emerge from commonly held values or themes from the past, institutional leaders searching for a unifying vision must be aware of the history and traditions that have guided their institution (Ratcliff 1989; Townsend 1986). They also should comprehend the college or university's current culture—not only to lead the organization more effectively (Bensimon 1990; Chaffee and Tierney 1988), but also to ascertain if its existing "shared values, assumptions, beliefs, and ideologies that members have about their organization or its work" reflect a distinctive educational vision (Peterson and Spencer 1990). The works of Masland (1985) and Tierney (1988; 1990) are excellent resources for those interested in researching their school's culture.

2. *Make a paradigm check.* Success in implementing a strategy leading to institutional distinctiveness likely will require using the tools of both the adaptive and the interpretive paradigms.

   Leaders first must become educated about the differences between the two paradigms and the types of action that each one uses. We suggest reading the works of Chaffee (1984; 1985), Grabowski (1981), and Hossler and

Bean (1990) for basic information about these strategies.

Next, leaders need to become aware of personal and institutional positions about management. Do actions—their own and those of other institutional leaders—tend to be guided by the adaptive or the interpretive models? We believe that the decisionmaking process of the distinctive college or university reflects the interpretive model. But, implementation of the distinctiveness strategy will use tools from the adaptive model. Success probably is most advanced when initiators of the strategy for institutional distinctiveness are grounded philosophically in the interpretive paradigm but pragmatically equipped with the tools of the adaptive paradigm.

3. *Clarify, communicate, and operationalize unifying values and themes.* There is no single clear path to the articulation and sharing of institutional values. They may be pronounced by the president in a time when direction is demanded. They may come from a societal cry for change that rallies internal constituents. They may emerge from long and painful debate over the future of the institution. They even may be written as promotional rhetoric that comes over time to be believed by constituents and becomes a reality. Normally, however, there will be key individuals or a small group which leads the school's community in discussing and then adopting the virtues around which institutional activities will be organized (Clark 1970).

Leaders also must make sure that the educational vision guiding and motivating internal constituents is operationalized in the curriculum and culture. A distinctive college or university becomes reality only when the set of unifying values is used to guide and direct the academic enterprise. In matters about general education, majors, course content, faculty selection, new programs, and program terminations, a primary concern must be how the distinctive vision and values are embodied in these activities. The imprint of the mission is seen in the norms and expectations that become the institutional culture (Clark 1970).

4. *Conduct a situation analysis.* Being a distinctive college or university is not without peril, as we have noted in previous sections. Leaders need to determine whether the school's situation presents a viable opportunity to develop distinctiveness. They should use the adaptive management

tool of situation analysis to consider the current position of the institution, threats and opportunities in the societal environment, strengths and limitations in the internal environment, and the institution's position relative to other colleges or universities of its type. See Kotler (1991) and Stevens, Loudon, and Warren (1992) for information about situation analysis.

5. *Select the desired level of market exposure.* Turning to the Porter Generic Model, institutional leaders may decide to position their college or university on the basis of its distinctive elements and gain broad regional or national favor. If the elements of distinctiveness can be positioned as having relevance to the general population, the school will build a national reputation that will likely increase its applicants, donations, and employment appeal.

However, the values producing distinctiveness need not have broad, national appeal. As long as they are relevant to a specific external constituency that sees economic value in the cause, a college or university can be extremely successful.

Thus, the Porter Generic Model suggests that striving for comprehensiveness may not enhance an institution's ability to survive in tough times. By producing an educational product that has specific merit to a narrow constituency, the distinctive college or university may be more likely to survive and even thrive.

6. *Execute market research and implement appropriate strategy.* Market research required at this point is different from that executed in the differentiation strategy. If executing a differentiation strategy, institutional leaders would use market research to detect external needs. These needs then would help define institutional mission, shape the educational product, and inform tactical decisions (such as pricing, delivery systems, and promotional strategy).

In the case of distinctive institutions, market research may uncover needs inconsistent with existing institutional values. These needs would be ignored. If the research uncovers needs consistent with institutional values, then further research would be conducted to provide insights about the appropriate pricing strategy, whether it is the low cost leader or the differentiated (premium priced) option.

Awareness of the market that the distinctive educational product is targeted to serve also can help shape the appropriate delivery system and promotional strategy. At this point, leaders are employing the mindset of adaptive strategic management to increase the probability that the distinctive school will find a market ready and willing to endorse its special contribution.

Institutional and system leaders desirous of developing and marketing more distinctive colleges and universities can use the tools of the adaptive model of strategic management to determine the viability of a strategy of institutional distinctiveness. This strategy, however, is ultimately based in the interpretive model of management.

Areas for Research

Researchers can play an important role in providing the information institutional and system leaders need to assess the likelihood that a specific college or university is distinctive and the constituencies who may value its distinctiveness. As we recommended above, in colleges or universities in which a conscious, planned movement to uncover or emphasize distinctiveness is contemplated, a situation analysis, a historical analysis, and a cultural analysis must be conducted. Institutional researchers presumably will conduct these. We also need the data provided by institutional and other researchers to develop a more comprehensive understanding of the phenomenon of institutional distinctiveness.

As part of the cultural analysis, institutional researchers will ask internal constituents their perceptions of the college or university (Townsend 1989b). If these perceptions are strong enough, they also can influence the perceptions of those outside the school. However, "organizational participants may have internalized attitudinal sets which are at substantial variance with those commonly held by more objective observers in the external organizational environment" (Leister and Maclachlan 1975, p. 211).

Those within an institution may view it as very distinctive, even though external constituencies do not. Leaders interested in developing a distinctive college or university may become misled into thinking they have done so if they rely only or primarily on internal perceptions. Therefore, it is vital that institutional researchers also conduct studies of external constituents' perceptions of the school.

Institutional researchers also should conduct retention studies. Generally, the more selective a college or university, the higher its retention rate (Tinto 1987). Given that many distinctive institutions are highly selective, they might be expected to sustain high retention rates. However, some evidence suggests that highly distinctive schools have a high dropout rate, especially during the freshman and sophomore years (Coyne and Hebert 1971-72; Grant and Riesman 1978; Meister 1982; Meyer 1992).

As in selecting a distinctive institution, attending one that expects atypical student behavior and academic performance may be more appealing in theory than in practice. Retention rates of institutions commonly viewed as distinctive need to be determined and compared with those of differentiated but not distinctive colleges and universities.

The value of attending a distinctive college or university also needs study. Do students who attend or have attended such distinctive institutions as Brooklyn College, Berea, Miami-Dade, or Deep Springs benefit in ways beyond those normally attributed to college attendance? If there are benefits, are they correlated with the degree of a school's distinctiveness or with the characteristics of small size and selectivity often associated with distinctive colleges? Grant and Riesman (1978) raised this issue in their discussion of St. John's, but concluded that "the data that are available do not enable one to make judgments about the virtues of St. John's graduates" (p. 71).

Evidence about the effect of college environment on psychosocial outcomes suggests that the overt value orientation of distinctive colleges and universities would have a positive effect on students' and graduates' "developmentally oriented outcomes" (Pascarella and Terenzini 1991, p. 592). Research focusing on the effects of attending distinctive colleges and universities needs to be conducted to determine if there are effects beyond those associated simply with college attendance and if these effects endure after students leave the school.

As more and more institutional leaders and researchers commit to an examination of their college's or university's past, culture, and perceptions of distinctiveness among various constituencies, those responsible for institutional leadership will have the information they need to work toward an institutional excellence that will benefit higher education as a whole. Also, this research will contribute to a data base which will enable us to understand better the temporal nature of distinctiveness.

This same data base also can serve to enhance our knowledge about distinctiveness across institutional types. Given that the majority of research has focused on small liberal arts colleges, we need research on other institutional types to develop a more precise definition that accounts for variations in distinctiveness according to institutional type and sector. We need to know if comprehensive colleges or universities can develop distinctiveness to a degree as high as that at liberal arts colleges. Is institutional size an intervening variable regardless of institutional type? How likely is institutional distinctiveness for a commuter college or university? These and other questions need to be answered to further our understanding of the phenomenon of institutional distinctiveness.

Summary

Based on a synthesis and evaluation of various literature bases, we have developed a definition of institutional distinctiveness and specified a plan for leaders to use in deciding whether to emphasize institutional distinctiveness as a viable strategy. Using the definition we developed, both college and university leaders and researchers can better assess the distinctive nature of individual colleges and universities. Using our plan, they can be better poised to assess and advance the truly distinctive qualities of their schools.

To move beyond this stage of analysis requires further research. We need to understand better the dynamics of distinctiveness to enhance our conception of what it is and how it is developed. We anticipate that this monograph will help clarify the concept of institutional distinctiveness and prompt further research on the topic.

A final comment: Even though we have presented evidence to indicate that distinctive colleges and universities often fail to endure or become less distinctive to survive, we hope this evidence will not discourage institutional and system leaders from envisioning distinctive schools and working to implement them.

Higher education is in need of visions. We urge educators— faculty, staff, administration, and system leaders—to commit to a cherished value or a compelling vision and then to articulate a purpose that challenges the commitment of others.

We urge educators— faculty, staff, administration, and system leaders—to commit to a cherished value or a compelling vision and then to articulate a purpose that challenges the commitment of others.

The callings, causes, and cries that make up the innermost commitments of people can become educational missions that chart new paths for higher education.

A few groundbreakers are necessary to lead the way. These individuals plant the seeds of innovation and distinctiveness. Their labor bears fruit for all of higher education.

REFERENCES

The Educational Resources Information Center (ERIC) Clearinghouse on Higher Education abstracts and indexes the current literature on higher education for inclusion in ERIC's data base and announcement in ERIC's monthly bibliographic journal, *Resources in Education* (RIE). Most of these publications are available through the ERIC Document Reproduction Service (EDRS). For publications cited in this bibliography that are available from EDRS, ordering number and price code are included. Readers who wish to order a publication should write to the ERIC Document Reproduction Service, 7420 Fullerton Rd., Suite 110, Springfield, VA 22153-2852. (Phone orders with VISA or MasterCard are taken at 800-443-ERIC or 703-440-1400.) When ordering, please specify the document (ED) number. Documents are available as noted in microfiche (MF) and paper copy (PC). If you have the price code ready when you call EDRS, an exact price can be quoted. The last page of the latest issue of *Resources in Education* also has the current cost, listed by code.

Adamic, Louis. 1938. *My America.* New York: Harper & Brothers.

Adams, William D. May/June 1984. "Getting Real: Santa Cruz and the Crisis of Liberal Education." *Change* 16: 19-27.

Alpert, Daniel. May/June 1986. "Performance and Paralysis: The Organizational Context of the American Research University." *Journal of Higher Education* 56(3): 241-81.

America's Best Colleges 1991. 1991. *U.S. News & World Report.*

Anderson, Richard E. January/February 1978. "A Financial and Environmental Analysis of Strategic Policy Changes at Small Private Colleges." *Journal of Higher Education 49: 30-45.*

Antioch College Catalog: 1990-1991. 1990. Yellow Springs, Ohio: Antioch Publications.

Aronow, B. 1983. *Such a Frail Bark: An Oral History of College of the Atlantic's Early Years.* Bar Harbor, Me.: College of the Atlantic.

Barrett, Laurence. Winter 1990. "Betting the Store: The K Plan Nears 30." *Kalamazoo College Quarterly* 52: 2-10.

Bennett, William J. November 28, 1984. " 'To Reclaim a Legacy': Text of Report on Humanities in Education." *Chronicle of Higher Education*: 16-21.

Bensimon, Estela Mara. Winter 1990. "The New President and Understanding the Campus as a Culture." In *Assessing Academic Climates and Cultures.* William G. Tierney, ed. New Directions for Institutional Research No. 68. San Francisco: Jossey-Bass.

Bentley, Eric R. Summer 1945. "Report from the Academy: The Experimental College." *Partisan Review* 12.

Biemiller, Lawrence. September 4, 1985. "Warren Wilson: Liberal Arts Plus Snapping Beans, Raising Pigs." *Chronicle of Higher Education*: 5.

―――. November 14, 1988. "Evergreen State College Still Eschews Grades and Tenure, Now Flirts with Prosperity." *Chronicle of*

Higher Education: 11-12.

Birnbaum, Robert. 1983. *Maintaining Diversity in Higher Education.* San Francisco: Jossey-Bass.

―――. 1992. *How Academic Leadership Works: Understanding Success and Failure in the College Presidency.* San Francisco: Jossey-Bass.

Boroff, David. 1961. *Campus U.S.A.: Portraits of American Colleges in Action.* New York: Harper & Brothers.

―――. March 23, 1963. "Four Years with the Great Books." *The Saturday Review*: 58-62.

Boulding, Kenneth E. 1961. *The Image: Knowledge in Life and Society.* Ann Arbor: University of Michigan Press.

Bowles, F., and F.A. DeCosta. 1971. *Between Two Worlds: A Profile of Negro Higher Education.* New York: McGraw-Hill.

Brann, Eva T. Summer 1984. "The Program of St. John's College." *The St. John's Review*: 48-55.

Breiseth, Christopher N. September 1983. "Deep Spring College: 'Learning to Hear the Voice of the Desert.'" *Change* 15: 28-35.

Breneman, David W. Summer 1990. "Are We Losing Our Liberal Arts Colleges?" *College Board Review* 156: 16-21+.

Brubacher, John S., and W. Rudy. 1976. *Higher Education in Transition: A History of American Colleges and Universities, 1636-1976.* 3rd ed. New York: Harper and Row.

Buchanan, William. 1985. "Educational Rebels in the Nineteen Thirties." *Journal of General Education* 37.

Butler, Addie Louise Joyner. 1977. *The Distinctive Black College: Talladega, Tuskegee and Morehouse.* Metuchen, N.J.: The Scarecrow Press, Inc.

Cable, Nancy Jane. 1984. "The Search for Mission in Ohio Liberal Arts Colleges: Denison, Kenyon, Marietta, Oberlin, 1870-1914." Ph.D. dissertation, University of Virginia.

Cadwallader, Mervyn. 1984. "The Uses of Philosophy in an Academic Counterrevolution." *Liberal Education* 70.

Cameron, Kim S. March/April 1984. "Organizational Adaptation and Higher Education." *Journal of Higher Education* 55: 122-44.

Carnegie Council on Policy Studies in Higher Education. 1980. *Three Thousand Futures: The Next Twenty Years for Higher Education.* San Francisco: Jossey-Bass.

Catalog: 1990-91. 1990. Brewer, Me.: College of the Atlantic.

Chaffee, Ellen Earle. March/April 1984. "Successful Strategic Management in Small Private Liberal Arts Colleges." *Journal of Higher Education* 55: 212- 32.

―――, and W.G. Tierney. 1988. *Collegiate Culture and Leadership Strategies.* New York: American Council on Education and Macmillan.

Chamberlain, Philip C. July/August 1985. "That Special Something: How Can You Identify What Makes Your Institution Distinctive?"

Case Currents. 14, 16.

Clark, Burton R. 1968. "College Image and Student Selection." In *The College Student and His Culture: An Analysis.* K. Yamamoto, ed. Boston: Houghton Mifflin.

———. 1970. *The Distinctive College: Reed, Antioch, & Swarthmore. College of the Atlantic Catalog.* 1990-91. Chicago: Aldine.

Clive, John, and Thomas Pinney, eds. 1972. *Thomas Babington Macaulay: Selected Writings.* Chicago: The University of Chicago Press.

Collins, Robert G. November 1969. "Notes on the Parsons Experience." *Journal of Higher Education* 38: 428-37.

Coyne, John, and Thomas Hebert. Winter 1971-72. "Goddard College: A Fresh Look at an Old Innovator." *Change* 3: 46-51.

Darkey, William, ed. 1979. *Three Dialogues on Liberal Education.* Annapolis, Md.: The St. John's College Press.

Dawson, Fielding. 1970. *The Black Mountain Book.* New York: Croton Press.

DeLoughry, T.J. January 22, 1992. "A Non-Traditional University Looks at Tradition." *Chronicle of Higher Education.* A5.

Dilts, Susan, ed. 1991. *Peterson's Guide to Four-Year Colleges.* Princeton, N.J.: Peterson's Guides.

Dixon, Terry. 1983. "Parsons College: Innovative Ideas or Unethical Practices." ED 239 534. 11 pp. MF-01; PC-01.

Duberman, Martin. 1972. *Black Mountain.* New York: E.P. Dutton.

Dzierlendga, Donna. 1981. "Sources and Information: Women in the Community College." In *Women in Community Colleges.* Judith S. Eaton, ed. New Directions for Community Colleges No. 34. San Francisco: Jossey-Bass.

Elmhurst College 1989-91 Catalog. 1989. Elmhurst College, Ill.

Ewell, Peter T., and R.P. Lisensky. 1988. *Assessing Institutional Effectiveness: Redirecting the Self-Study Process.* Consortium for the Advancement of Private Higher Education.

Gallaudet University. n.d. Washington, D.C.

Gamson, Zelda F., and Associates. 1984. *Liberating Education.* San Francisco: Jossey-Bass.

Geiger, Roger L. 1986. *To Advance Knowledge: The Growth of American Research Universities, 1900-1940.* New York: Oxford University Press.

Grabowski, Stanley M. 1981. *Marketing in Higher Education.* ASHE-ERIC Higher Education Research Report No. 5. Washington, D.C.: Association for the Study of Higher Education. ED 214 445. pp. 47. MF-01; PC-02.

Grant, Gerald, and Associates. 1979. *On Competence.* San Francisco: Jossey-Bass.

Grant, Gerald, and D. Riesman. 1978. *The Perpetual Dream: Reform and Experiment in the American College.* Chicago: University of Chicago Press.

Greene, Elizabeth. September 2, 1987. "Five Colleges to Study Benefits of Requiring Students to Hold Campus Jobs." *Chronicle of Higher Education*: A86.

Hampshire College 1992 Undergraduate Catalogue. 1992. Amherst, Mass.

Hankin, Joseph. 1989. "What Makes the Community College Distinctive." In *A Search for Institutional Distinctiveness.* Barbara K. Townsend, ed. New Directions for Community Colleges No. 65. San Francisco: Jossey-Bass.

Harris, Mary E. 1987. *The Arts at Black Mountain College.* Boston: MIT Press.

Heller, Scott. February 26, 1992. "U. of Chicago at 100: Proud Traditionalist." *Chronicle of Higher Education*: A18-19+.

Henderson, Algo D., and D. Hall. 1946. *Antioch College: Its Design for Liberal Education.* New York: Harper & Brothers.

Herman, Martin. February 20, 1992. Telephone conversation with humanities chair at Wayne State University.

Hesburgh, Theodore M. October 1983. "Preparing for the Millenium: Finding an Identity and a Future." *Change* 15: 14-17.

Hess, Robert. 1985. "Brooklyn College: Through Adversity to Excellence." In *Opportunity in Adversity: How Colleges Can Succeed in Hard Times.* Janice Green and Arthur Levine, eds. San Francisco: Jossey-Bass.

Hossler, Don. 1984. *Enrollment Management: An Integrated Approach.* New York: College Entrance Examination Board.

———. 1986. Creating Effective Enrollment Management Systems. New York: College Entrance Examination Board.

Hossler, Don, and J.P. Bean. 1990. *The Strategic Management of College Enrollments.* San Francisco: Jossey-Bass.

Hutchins, Francis S. 1963. *Berea College: The Telescope and the Spade.* New York: Newcomen Society in North America.

Hutchins, Robert Maynard. January 1934. "The Issue in the Higher Learning." *The International Journal of Ethics*: 175-84.

———. 1936. The Higher Learning in America. New Haven, Conn.: Yale University Press.

Jencks, Christopher, and D. Riesman. 1968. *The Academic Revolution.* Garden City, N.Y.: Doubleday.

Jones, Richard M. 1981. *Experiment at Evergreen.* Cambridge, Mass.: Schenkman Publications.

———, and B.L. Smith. 1984. *Across the Current.* Cambridge, Mass.: Schenkman Publications.

Kaplan, William A. 1979. *The Law of Higher Education.* San Francisco: Jossey-Bass.

Kaufman, Herbert. 1991. *Time, Chance, and Organizations: Natural Selection in a Perilous Environment.* 2nd ed. Chatham, N.J.: Chatham House Publishers Inc.

Keeley, Michael. 1988. *A Social-Contract Theory of Organizations.*

Notre Dame, Ind.: University of Notre Dame Press.

Keller, George. 1983. *Academic Strategy: The Management Revolution in American Higher Education*. Baltimore: Johns Hopkins Press.

Kemerer, Frank, V. Baldridge, and K. Green. 1982. *Strategies for Effective Enrollment Management*. Washington, D.C.: American Association of State Colleges and Universities.

Kerr, Clark. 1982. *The Uses of the University*. Cambridge, Mass.: Harvard University Press.

Kirp, David L. February/March 1992. "Tales from the Bright Side: The Surprising Success of America's Biggest Community College." *Lingua franca* 1: 20-26.

Koerner, James D. July 19, 1969. "The Life and Hard Times of Parsons College." *Saturday Review*: 53-55+.

————. March/April 1971. "Preserving the Status Quo: Academia's Hidden Cartel." *Change*: 50-54.

Kotler, Philip. 1991. *Marketing Management: Analysis, Planning, Implementation, and Control*. Englewood Cliffs, N.J.: Prentice-Hall, Inc.

Kotler, Philip, and K. Fox. 1985. *Strategic Marketing for Educational Institutions*. Englewood Cliffs, N.J.: Prentice-Hall, Inc.

Kotler, Philip, and P.E. Murphy. September/October 1981. "Strategic Planning for Higher Education." *Journal of Higher Education* 52: 470-89.

Kuh, George D., and J.H. Schuh, eds. 1991. *The Role & Contribution of Student Affairs in Involving Colleges*. Washington, D.C.: National Association of Student Personnel Administrators Inc.

————, J.H. Schuh, E.J. Whitt, and Associates. 1991. *Involving Colleges: Successful Approach to Fostering Student Learning and Development Outside the Classroom*. San Francisco: Jossey-Bass.

————, and E.J. Whitt. 1988. *The Invisible Tapestry: Culture in American Colleges and Universities*. ASHE-ERIC Higher Education Report No. 1. Washington, D.C.: Association for the Study of Higher Education. ED 299 934. 160 pp. MF-01; PC-07.

Landmark College Catalogue 1989-91. 1989. Putney, Vt.

Lane, Mervin, ed. 1990. *Black Mountain College: Sprouted Seeds*. Knoxville: University of Tennessee Press.

Laramee, William A. Spring 1987. "The Role of Metaphors in Higher Education." *College Board Review* 143: 18-19+.

Leister, Douglas V., and D.L. Maclachlan. June 1975. "Organizational Self-Perception and Environmental Image Measurement." *Academy of Management Journal* 18: 205-23.

Levine, Arthur. 1978. *Handbook on Undergraduate Curriculum*. San Francisco: Jossey-Bass.

Lynton, Ernest A., and S.E. Elman. 1987. *New Priorities for the University*. San Francisco: Jossey-Bass.

Magner, Denise. February 1, 1989. "Milwaukee's Alverno College:

For 16 Years, a Pioneer in Weaning Students from Dependence on Teachers." *Chronicle of Higher Education*: 9+.

Martin, Warren Bryan. 1969. *Conformity: Standards and Change in Higher Education.* San Francisco: Jossey-Bass.

——. 1982. *College of Character: Renewing the Purpose and Content of College Education.* San Francisco: Jossey-Bass.

——. March/April 1984. "Adaptation and Distinctiveness." *Journal of Higher Education* 55: 286-96.

Martineau, P. 1957. *Motivation in Advertising.* New York: McGraw-Hill.

Martines, Lauro. Spring 1985. "Large and Little School Teaching." *The American Scholar* 54: 194-203.

Masland, Andrew T. 1985. "Organizational Culture in the Study of Higher Education." *Review of Higher Education* 8: 157-68.

Mayhew, Lewis B. May/June 1974. "The Steady Seventies." *Journal of Higher Education* 45: 163-74.

McCarthy, Coleman. September 15, 1990. "Learning to Learn." *The Washington Post*: 5.

Meiklejohn, Alexander. 1932. *The Experimental College.* Washington, D.C.: Seven Locks Press.

——. January 1945. "A Reply to John Dewey." *Fortune.*

Meister, Joel S. March 1982. "The Amherst and Hampshire Experiences." *Change* 14: 26-34.

Meyer, Marshall W., and L.G. Zucker. 1989. *Permanently Failing Organizations.* Newbury Park, Calif.: Sage Publications.

Meyer, Thomas J. January 15, 1986. "At America's Costliest College, Learning to Read is a Major Accomplishment." Chronicle of Higher Education: 2.

——. February/March 1992. "Reed Screed." *Lingua franca*: 10-11.

Millet, John D. 1985. "State Governments." In *Higher Education and American Society.* Philip G. Altach and Robert O. Berdahl, eds. Rev. ed. New York: Promotheus.

Moon, Peter. 1990. "The Need for a Human Ecological Perspective in Business: A Graduation Address." *The Peregrine: Newsletter of the College of the Atlantic*: 1-9.

Morgan, Anthony W., and L.J. Newell. Summer 1981. "Strategic Planning at a Small College: To be Comprehensive or to be Distinctive?" *Planning for Higher Education* 9: 29-33.

Morgan, Joy Elmer. 1938. *Horace Mann at Antioch.* Washington, D.C.: The Horace Mann Centennial Fund, National Education Association.

Moseley, John D. 1988. "The President and the Role and Mission of the College." In *Courage in Mission: Presidential Leadership in the Church-Related College.* D.H. Dagley, ed. Washington, D.C.: Council for the Advancement and Support of Education. ED 299 869. 175 pp. MF-01; PC-07.

Newell, L. Jackson. Summer 1982. "Among the Few at Deep Springs

College: Assessing a Seven-Decade Experiment in Liberal Education." *The Journal of General Education* 34: 120-34.

"On the Green." 1989-90. Gallaudet University. Washington, D.C.

Pace, C. Robert. 1974. *The Demise of Diversity? A Comparative of Eight Types of Institutions.* Carnegie Foundation for the Advancement of Teaching.

Pascarella, Ernest T., and P.T. Terenzini. 1991. *How College Affects Students.* San Francisco: Jossey-Bass.

Peck, E.S. 1982. *Berea's First 125 Years: 1855-1980.* Lexington, Ky.: University Press of Kentucky.

Perus, Arumynayagam Malkia. 1978. *The Phasing Out of an Innovative Subcollege/Cluster College (Monteith College, Wayne State University): A Case Study in Conflict Dynamics.* Ph.D. dissertation, Bowling Green State University.

Peterson, Marvin W., and M.G. Spencer. 1990. "Understanding Academic Culture and Climate." In *Assessing Academic Climates and Cultures.* William G. Tierney, ed. New Directions for Institutional Research No. 68. San Francisco: Jossey-Bass.

Pfeffer, J. 1981. "Management as Symbolic Action." In *Research in Organizational Behavior* 3: 12-52. L.L. Cummings and B.M. Staw, eds. Greenwich, Conn.: JAI Press.

Porter, Michael. E. 1980. *Competitive Strategy: Techniques for Analyzing Industries and Competitors.* New York: Free Press.

———. 1985. *Competitive Advantage: Creating and Sustaining Superior Performance.* New York: Free Press.

Ratcliff, James L. 1989. "Getting the Facts, Analyzing the Data, Building the Case for Institutional Distinctiveness." In *A Search for Institutional Distinctiveness.* Barbara K. Townsend, ed. New Directions for Community Colleges No. 65. San Francisco: Jossey-Bass.

Read, Sister Joel, and S.R. Sharkey. 1985. "Alverno College: Toward a Community of Learning." In *Opportunity in Adversity: How Colleges Can Succeed in Hard Times.* Janice Green and Arthur Levine, eds. San Francisco: Jossey-Bass.

Reed College Catalog. 1990. Portland, Ore.: Reed College Publications.

Reed College Self-Evaluation Report, Vol. II. 1958. Portland, Ore.: Reed College Publications.

Rice, John A. May 1937. "Fundamentalism and the Higher Learning." *Harpers.* 174.

Rice, R. Eugene, and A.E. Austin. March/April 1988. "High Faculty Morale: What Exemplary Colleges Do Right." *Change.* 50-58.

Richman, Barry M., and R. Farmer. 1976. *Leadership, Goals, and Power in Higher Education.* San Francisco: Jossey-Bass.

Riesman, David. 1980. *On Higher Education: The Academic Enterprise in an Era of Rising Student Consumerism.* San Francisco: Jossey-Bass.

———, J. Gusfield, and Z. Gamson. 1970. *Values and Mass Education: The Early Years of Oakland and Monteith.* Garden City, N.Y.:

Doubleday.

Ritz, Richard E. 1990. *A History of the Reed College Campus and Its Buildings.* Portland, Ore.: Reed College Publications.

Rossman, J.E., and E. El-Khawas. 1987. *Thinking about Assessment: Perspectives for Presidents and Chief Academic Officers.* Washington, D.C.: American Council of Education and American Association for Higher Education. ED 292 433. 28 pp. MF-01; PC-02.

Rouche, John E., and G.A. Baker III. 1987. *Access and Excellence: The Open-Door College.* Washington, D.C.: Community College Press.

Rowe, Roberta Lynn. 1980. "A Case Study of Maharishi International University: An Innovative Institution of Higher Education." Ed.D. dissertation, University of California, Santa Barbara.

Rudolph, Frederick. 1977. *Curriculum: A History of the Undergraduate Course of Study Since 1636.* San Francisco: Jossey-Bass.

St. John's College Catalog, 1990-1991. 1990. Annapolis, Md.: St. John's College.

Schein, Edgar H. 1985. *Organizational Culture and Leadership.* San Francisco: Jossey-Bass.

Skolnik, Michael. November/December 1989. "How Academic Program Review Can Foster Intellectual Conformity and Stifle Diversity of Thought and Method." *Journal of Higher Education* 60: 619-43.

Smirich, Linda, and G. Morgan. 1982. "Leadership: The Management of Meaning." *Journal of Applied Behavioral Science* 18: 257-73.

Smith, Daryl G. March/April 1990. "Women's Colleges and Coed Colleges: Is There a Difference for Women?" *Journal of Higher Education* 61: 181-95.

Smith, Emily Ann. November/December 1982. "Educating Head & Hands." *Change* 14: 32-37.

Smith, Louis. Spring 1950. "Berea College Will Enroll Negro Students from the Southern Mountain Region." *Mountain Life and Work* 26: 23.

Smith, Russell T. 1980. "Distinctive Traditions at the College of William and Mary and Their Influence on the Modernization of the College, 1865 to 1919." Ed.D. dissertation, College of William and Mary.

Stevens, Robert E., D.I. Loudon, and W.E. Warren. 1992. *Marketing Planning Guide.* Binghamton, N.Y.: Haworth Press.

Sutton, H.L. 1959. "The Humanities—Campus-Wide: A Description of the Humanities Program at Parson College." *Journal of Higher Education* 12: 151-57.

Templin, Robert. 1989. "Using What an Institution Learns in the Search for Distinctiveness." In *A Search for Institutional Distinctiveness.* Barbara K. Townsend, ed. New Directions for Community Colleges No. 65. San Francisco: Jossey-Bass.

Tierney, William G. January/February 1988. "Organizational Culture in Higher Education: Defining the Essentials." *Journal of Higher Education* 59: 2-21.

———. 1989. "Ideology and Identity in Postsecondary Institutions. Paper presented at the annual meeting of the Association for the Study of Higher Education. Atlanta, Ga.

———, ed. 1990. *Assessing Academic Climates and Cultures.* New Directions for Institutional Research No. 68. San Francisco: Jossey-Bass.

Tilghman, Tench F. 1984. *The Early History of St. John's College in Annapolis.* Annapolis, Md.: St. John's College Press.

Tinto, Vincent. 1987. *Leaving College: Rethinking the Causes of Student Attrition.* Chicago: University of Chicago Press.

Townsend, Barbara K. August/September 1986. "Past as Prologue: Seeds of an Institution's Identity." *Community Junior College Journal:* 46-49.

———, ed. 1989a. *A Search for Institutional Distinctiveness.* New Directions for Community Colleges No. 65. San Francisco: Jossey-Bass.

———. 1989b. "A Search for Institutional Distinctiveness: Overview of Process and Possibilities." In *Search for Institutional Distinctiveness.* Barbara K. Townsend, ed. New Directions for Community Colleges No. 65. San Francisco: Jossey-Bass.

Trow, Martin A. 1984. "The Analysis of States." In *Perspectives on Higher Education: Eight Disciplinary and Comparative Views.* Burton R. Clark, ed. Berkeley: University of California Press.

Tussman, Joseph. 1969. *Experiment at Berkeley.* New York: Oxford University Press.

———. 1984. "Remembering Alexander Meiklejohn." *Liberal Education* 70: 323-42.

Van Dyne, Larry. May 27, 1973. "On the Campuses." *Chronicle of Higher Education:* 4.

Wald, Matthew L. March 25, 1986. "Dyslexics Learn College Skills." *The New York Times:* C1+.

Ward, F. Champion. 1950. *The Idea and Practice of General Education.* Chicago: The University of Chicago Press.

Watts, Andre G. 1972. *Diversity and Choice in Higher Education.* London: Routledge & Kegan Paul.

Whitehead, John S., J. Herbst, and D.B. Potts. 1991. "Celebrating Roots: Sesquicentennials and the Distinctiveness of the Liberal Arts College." *History of Higher Education Annual* II: 7-19.

Willie, Charles V., and R.R. Edmonds. 1978. *Black Colleges in America: Challenge, Development, Survival.* New York: Teachers College Press.

Zoffer, H.J. Winter 1987. "Accreditation Bends Before the Winds of Change." *Educational Record:* 43-44.

Zwerling, L. Stephen. January/February 1988. "The Miami-Dade Story: Is It Really Number One?" Change 20: 10-23.

INDEX

A

Academic departments absent, 29, 30, 36, 42
Adaptive Strategy, 49, 61, 67
        in Business, 50-52
        in Higher Education, 52-55
admissions standards
        moderately selective, 7
        high, 8
        highly selective colleges, 8, 21
Albers, Josef, 27
Alverno College, 8-9, 12, 37, 57, 60
American Association of University Professors, 26
Amherst College, 23, 28, 46-47
Antioch College, 16-18, 56
Antioch University. See Antioch College.
Appalachian students, 19
Asheville Farm School. See Warren Wilson College
assessment model, 9
Aydolette, Frank, 26

B

Barr, Stringfellow, 28, 36
benefits of attending, 68
Berea College, 18-19, 24, 35, 37, 60
Birnbaum on values, 4-5
black
        colleges, 3, 5-6
        students, 18-19
Black Mountain College, 26-27, 59, 64
        alumni reunion in San Francisco, 27
        farm labour program failure, 26
Brewer, Les, 31
Brooklyn College, 7-8, 57, 60
Buchanan, Scott, 28, 36
Bunker Hill Community College, 5, 60

C

Caldwallader, Mervyn, 30
Cambridge University, 1
career education
        for, 44
        absence of, 29
Central American students. See scholarships for
Chicago Plan, 25, 28
Clay, Cassius M., 18
College of the Atlantic, 31-33, 35, 36, 59
College of William and Mary, 40
co-education, 17,18

---

human ecology, 32, 35, 59

I

illusion of distinctiveness, 63
images of fact, 10
institutional
       environment adaptation, 35
       definitions standardized, 45
       excellence, 8, 12
       high academic standards, 20
       homogeneity, 1
       size as a variable, 69
       types, 3
intercollegiate athletics absence, 20, 43
internal constituents, 4
Interpretive Model, 49-50, 58, 60, 67
Interpretive paradigm. See Interpretive Model

J

Jewish student body, 7
John F. Kennedy University, 44-45

K

Kaelber   Edward, 32
Kalamazoo College, 38, 60
Kerr, Clark, 24
King William's School. See St. John's College

L

Landmark College, 11-12, 57, 60
leadership promise criteria, 21
learning
       disabilities. See Landmark College and Gallaudet University
       groups, 30. See also University of Wisconsin
liberal arts
       colleges, 3, 9
       education, 20, 25, 38, 43, 47
       experience, 8
       private colleges, 6, 56
liberal education undergraduate emphasis, 45
London University, 1
low cost, 60, 66. See also Porter generic Model
Lynd, Helen, 28

M

Maharishi International University, 37
Mann, Horace, 16
market exposure, 66

Rice, John Andrew, 26-27
Riesman, David, 34
Roberts, Millard G., 40-41
Rollins College, 26

S

St. John's College, 27-29, 35-36, 37, 57, 68
    Santa Fe campus, 29
San Jose College, 54
scholarships for Central American students, 5
Science of Creative Intelligence, 37
situation analysis, 65-66
small classes and discussions, 20
Smith College, 58
special calling, 37
Stanford, Leland, 56
State University of New York at Stony Brook, 58
Strategic Management, 49
structuring educational content and learning, 22, 29
students
    academically gifted, 17, 21, 55
    academically talented tuition absence, 7
    academically weak, 41
    campus governance participation, 9, 17, 20, 21, 45
    Central American. See scholarships for
    no tuition for, 7
    non-traditional, 54
    part-time, 54
study abroad
    opportunity, 5
    requirement, 38
Study of Human Consciousness, 44
Swarthmore, 26, 56, 57, 60

T

Talladega College, 5-6
telic reforms, 34, 47
teaching chairs, 60
teaching
    effectiveness, 60
    innovative support, 25
    interactive methods, 17, 26
transcendental meditation, 37
Tussman, Joseph, 30, 36

U

University High School, 25

University of
>California at Berkeley, 23, 24, 30
>California at Santa Cruz, 45-46, 64
>Chicago, 7, 22-25, 64
>Virginia, 28
>Wisconsin, 23

V

values
>commitment to shared, 5
>confusion over, 2
>images of, 10
>institutional, 4, 64
>shared institutional necessary, 10
>system of institution, 4-5, 10
>unifying theme, ideology or system, 6-7

vision
>as aid to decisionmaking, 38
>clarity, xv
>implementation of, 65
>motivating force, xv, 61-62, 63
>value, 69

W

Warren Wilson College, 6
Wayne State University, 42
Western Association of Schools and Colleges, 44
Western Washington University, 34
Western College Program, 34
Wheaton College, 55
William Jewel, 58
women's colleges, 3, 8. See also female student body.,
woodworking, 18
work-study programs. See community service requirement.

Y

Yale, 24

ASHE-ERIC HIGHER EDUCATION REPORTS

Since 1983, the Association for the Study of Higher Education (ASHE) and the Educational Resources Information Center (ERIC) Clearinghouse on Higher Education, a sponsored project of the School of Education and Human Development at The George Washington University, have cosponsored the *ASHE-ERIC Higher Education Report* series. The 1992 series is the twenty-first overall and the fourth to be published by the School of Education and Human Development at the George Washington University.

Each monograph is the definitive analysis of a tough higher education problem, based on thorough research of pertinent literature and institutional experiences. Topics are identified by a national survey. Noted practitioners and scholars are then commissioned to write the reports, with experts providing critical reviews of each manuscript before publication.

Eight monographs (10 before 1985) in the ASHE-ERIC Higher Education Report series are published each year and are available on individual and subscription bases. Subscription to eight issues is $90.00 annually; $70 to members of AAHE, AIR, or AERA; and $60 to ASHE members. All foreign subscribers must include an additional $10 per series year for postage.

To order single copies of existing reports, use the order form on the last page of this book. Regular prices, and special rates available to members of AAHE, AIR, AERA and ASHE, are as follows:

Series	Regular	Members
1990 to 92	$17.00	$12.75
1988 and 89	15.00	11.25
1985 to 87	10.00	7.50
1983 and 84	7.50	6.00
before 1983	6.50	5.00

Shipping costs are as follows:
- U.S. address: 5% of invoice subtotal for orders over $50.00; $2.50 for each order with an invoice subtotal of $50.00 or less.
- Foreign: $2.50 per book.

All orders under $45.00 must be prepaid. Make check payable to ASHE-ERIC. For Visa or MasterCard, include card number, expiration date and signature. A bulk discount of 10% is available on orders of 10 or more books, and 20% on orders of 25 or more books (not applicable on subscriptions).

Address order to
ASHE-ERIC Higher Education Reports
The George Washington University
1 Dupont Circle, Suite 630
Washington, DC 20036
Or phone (202) 296-2597
Write or call for a complete catalog.

1992 ASHE-ERIC Higher Education Reports

1. The Leadership Compass: Values and Ethics in Higher Education
   John R. Wilcox and Susan L. Ebbs

2. Preparing for a Global Community: Achieving an International Perspective in Higher Education
   Sarah M. Pickert

3. Quality: Transforming Postsecondary Education
   Ellen Earle Chaffee and Lawrence A. Sherr

4. Faculty Job Satisfaction: Women and Minorities in Peril
   Martha Wingard Tack and Carol Logan Patitu

5. Reconciling Rights and Responsibilities of Colleges and Students: Offensive Speech, Assembly, Drug Testing, and Safety
   Annette Gibbs

1991 ASHE-ERIC Higher Education Reports

1. Active Learning: Creating Excitement in the Classroom
   Charles C. Bonwell and James A. Eison

2. Realizing Gender Equality in Higher Education: The Need to Integrate Work/Family Issues
   Nancy Hensel

3. Academic Advising for Student Success: A System of Shared Responsibility
   Susan H. Frost

4. Cooperative Learning: Increasing College Faculty Instructional Productivity
   David W. Johnson, Roger T. Johnson, and Karl A. Smith

5. High School–College Partnerships: Conceptual Models, Programs, and Issues
   Arthur Richard Greenberg

6. Meeting the Mandate: Renewing the College and Departmental Curriculum
   William Toombs and William Tierney

7. Faculty Collaboration: Enhancing the Quality of Scholarship and Teaching
   Ann E. Austin and Roger G. Baldwin

8. Strategies and Consequences: Managing the Costs in Higher Education
   John S. Waggaman

1990 ASHE-ERIC Higher Education Reports

1. The Campus Green: Fund Raising in Higher Education
   Barbara E. Brittingham and Thomas R. Pezzullo

2. The Emeritus Professor: Old Rank - New Meaning
   James E. Mauch, Jack W. Birch, and Jack Matthews

3. "High Risk" Students in Higher Education: Future Trends
   Dionne J. Jones and Betty Collier Watson

4. Budgeting for Higher Education at the State Level: Enigma, Paradox, and Ritual
   Daniel T. Layzell and Jan W. Lyddon

5. Proprietary Schools: Programs, Policies, and Prospects
   John B. Lee and Jamie P. Merisotis

6. College Choice: Understanding Student Enrollment Behavior
   Michael B. Paulsen

7. Pursuing Diversity: Recruiting College Minority Students
   Barbara Astone and Elsa Nuñez-Wormack

8. Social Consciousness and Career Awareness: Emerging Link in Higher Education
   John S. Swift, Jr.

1989 ASHE-ERIC Higher Education Reports

1. Making Sense of Administrative Leadership: The 'L' Word in Higher Education
   Estela M. Bensimon, Anna Neumann, and Robert Birnbaum

2. Affirmative Rhetoric, Negative Action: African-American and Hispanic Faculty at Predominantly White Universities
   Valora Washington and William Harvey

3. Postsecondary Developmental Programs: A Traditional Agenda with New Imperatives
   Louise M. Tomlinson

4. The Old College Try: Balancing Athletics and Academics in Higher Education
   John R. Thelin and Lawrence L. Wiseman

5. The Challenge of Diversity: Involvement or Alienation in the Academy?
   Daryl G. Smith

6. Student Goals for College and Courses: A Missing Link in Assessing and Improving Academic Achievement
   Joan S. Stark, Kathleen M. Shaw, and Malcolm A. Lowther

7. The Student as Commuter: Developing a Comprehensive Institutional Response
   Barbara Jacoby

8. Renewing Civic Capacity: Preparing College Students for Service and Citizenship
   Suzanne W. Morse

1988 ASHE-ERIC Higher Education Reports

1. The Invisible Tapestry: Culture in American Colleges and Universities
   George D. Kuh and Elizabeth J. Whitt

2. Critical Thinking: Theory, Research, Practice, and Possibilities
   Joanne Gainen Kurfiss

3. Developing Academic Programs: The Climate for Innovation
   Daniel T. Seymour

4. Peer Teaching: To Teach is To Learn Twice
   Neal A. Whitman

5. Higher Education and State Governments: Renewed Partnership, Cooperation, or Competition?
   Edward R. Hines

6. Entrepreneurship and Higher Education: Lessons for Colleges, Universities, and Industry
   James S. Fairweather

7. Planning for Microcomputers in Higher Education: Strategies for the Next Generation
   Reynolds Ferrante, John Hayman, Mary Susan Carlson, and Harry Phillips

8. The Challenge for Research in Higher Education: Harmonizing Excellence and Utility
   Alan W. Lindsay and Ruth T. Neumann

1987 ASHE-ERIC Higher Education Reports

1. Incentive Early Retirement Programs for Faculty: Innovative Responses to a Changing Environment
   Jay L. Chronister and Thomas R. Kepple, Jr.

2. Working Effectively with Trustees: Building Cooperative Campus Leadership
   Barbara E. Taylor

3. Formal Recognition of Employer-Sponsored Instruction: Conflict and Collegiality in Postsecondary Education
   Nancy S. Nash and Elizabeth M. Hawthorne

4. Learning Styles: Implications for Improving Educational Practices
   Charles S. Claxton and Patricia H. Murrell

5. Higher Education Leadership: Enhancing Skills through Professional Development Programs
   Sharon A. McDade

6. Higher Education and the Public Trust: Improving Stature in Colleges and Universities
   Richard L. Alfred and Julie Weissman

7. College Student Outcomes Assessment: A Talent Development
Perspective
Maryann Jacobi, Alexander Astin, and Frank Ayala, Jr.

8. Opportunity from Strength: Strategic Planning Clarified with
Case Examples
Robert G. Cope

1986 ASHE-ERIC Higher Education Reports

1. Post-tenure Faculty Evaluation: Threat or Opportunity?
Christine M. Licata

2. Blue Ribbon Commissions and Higher Education: Changing
Academe from the Outside
Janet R. Johnson and Laurence R. Marcus

3. Responsive Professional Education: Balancing Outcomes and
Opportunities
Joan S. Stark, Malcolm A. Lowther, and Bonnie M.K. Hagerty

4. Increasing Students' Learning: A Faculty Guide to Reducing
Stress among Students
Neal A. Whitman, David C. Spendlove, and Claire H. Clark

5. Student Financial Aid and Women: Equity Dilemma?
Mary Moran

6. The Master's Degree: Tradition, Diversity, Innovation
Judith S. Glazer

7. The College, the Constitution, and the Consumer Student: Implications for Policy and Practice
Robert M. Hendrickson and Annette Gibbs

8. Selecting College and University Personnel: The Quest and
the Question
Richard A. Kaplowitz

1985 ASHE-ERIC Higher Education Reports

1. Flexibility in Academic Staffing: Effective Policies and Practices
*Kenneth P. Mortimer, Marque Bagshaw, and Andrew T.
Masland*

2. Associations in Action: The Washington, D.C. Higher Education
Community
Harland G. Bloland

3. And on the Seventh Day: Faculty Consulting and Supplemental
Income
Carol M. Boyer and Darrell R. Lewis

4. Faculty Research Performance: Lessons from the Sciences and
Social Sciences
John W. Creswell

5. Academic Program Review: Institutional Approaches, Expectations, and Controversies
   Clifton F. Conrad and Richard F. Wilson

6. Students in Urban Settings: Achieving the Baccalaureate Degree
   Richard C. Richardson, Jr. and Louis W. Bender

7. Serving More Than Students: A Critical Need for College Student Personnel Services
   Peter H. Garland

8. Faculty Participation in Decision Making: Necessity or Luxury?
   Carol E. Floyd

1984 ASHE-ERIC Higher Education Reports

1. Adult Learning: State Policies and Institutional Practices
   K. Patricia Cross and Anne-Marie McCartan

2. Student Stress: Effects and Solutions
   Neal A. Whitman, David C. Spendlove, and Claire H. Clark

3. Part-time Faulty: Higher Education at a Crossroads
   Judith M. Gappa

4. Sex Discrimination Law in Higher Education: The Lessons of the Past Decade. ED 252 169.*
   J. Ralph Lindgren, Patti T. Ota, Perry A. Zirkel, and Nan Van Gieson

5. Faculty Freedoms and Institutional Accountability: Interactions and Conflicts
   Steven G. Olswang and Barbara A. Lee

6. The High Technology Connection: Academic/Industrial Cooperation for Economic Growth
   Lynn G. Johnson

7. Employee Educational Programs: Implications for Industry and Higher Education. ED 258 501.*
   Suzanne W. Morse

8. Academic Libraries: The Changing Knowledge Centers of Colleges and Universities
   Barbara B. Moran

9. Futures Research and the Strategic Planning Process: Implications for Higher Education
   James L. Morrison, William L. Renfro, and Wayne I. Boucher

10. Faculty Workload: Research, Theory, and Interpretation
    Harold E. Yuker

*Out-of-print. Available through EDRS. Call 1-800-443-ERIC.

ORDER FORM

Quantity   **Amount**

_____ Please begin my subscription to the 1992 *ASHE-ERIC Higher Education Reports* at $90.00, 33% off the cover price, starting with Report 1, 1992.   _____

_____ Please send a complete set of the 1991 *ASHE-ERIC Higher Education Reports* at $80.00, 41% off the cover price.   _____

_____ Outside the U.S., add $10.00 per series for postage.   _____

Individual reports are avilable at the following prices:

1990 and 1991, $17.00	1983 and 1984, $7.50
1988 and 1989, $15.00	1982 and back, $6.50
1985 to 1987, $10.00	

Book rate postage within the U.S. is included. Outside U.S., please add $1.00 per book for postage. Fast U.P.S. shipping is available within the contiguous U.S. at $2.50 for each order under $50.00, and calculated at 5% of invoice total for orders $50.00 or above. All orders under $45.00 must be prepaid.

PLEASE SEND ME THE FOLLOWING REPORTS:

Quantity	Report No.	Year	Title	Amount

Subtotal:	
Foreign or UPS:	
Total Due:	

Please check one of the following:
☐ Check enclosed, payable to GWU–ERIC.
☐ Purchase order attached ($45.00 minimum).
☐ Charge my credit card indicated below:
   ☐ Visa   ☐ MasterCard

Expiration Date _____

Name _____

Title _____

Institution _____

Address _____

City _____ State _____ Zip _____

Phone _____

Signature _____ Date _____

SEND ALL ORDERS TO:
ASHE-ERIC Higher Education Reports
The George Washington University
One Dupont Circle, Suite 630
Washington, DC 20036-1183
Phone: (202) 296-2597